AN INTRODUCTION TO

VIKING
MYTHOLOGY

AN INTRODUCTION TO

VIKING MYTHOLOGY

JOHN GRANT

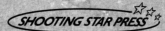
SHOOTING STAR PRESS

A QUANTUM BOOK

Published by Shooting Star Press, Inc.
230 Fifth Avenue, Suite 1212
New York, NY 10001
USA

ISBN 1-57335-315-9

This book was produced by
Quantum Books Ltd
6 Blundell Street
London N7 9BH

Creative Director: Peter Bridgewater
Art Director: Terry Jeavons
Designer: Sally McKay
Project Editor: Caroline Beattie
Editor: Susan Baker
Picture Researcher: Jon Newman
Illustrator: Lorraine Harrison

Typeset in Great Britain by
Central Southern Typesetters, Eastbourne
Manufactured in Hong Kong by
Regent Publishing Services Limited
Printed in Singapore by
Star Standard Industries (Pte) Ltd.

Contents

INTRODUCTION

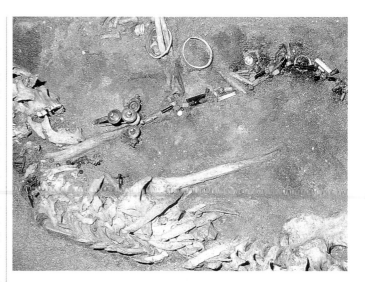

Viking mythology is Norse mythology, and Norse mythology is in turn the best recorded version of Teutonic mythology. It seems fitting that the main records we have of the Viking myths come from an outpost, Iceland.

The Vikings were a Teutonic people who established themselves in Scandinavia between the late 8th century and the middle of the 11th century. They were characterized by a mixture of great chivalry and barbaric cruelty. They pillaged the eastern coastline of mainland Britain, killing men and children and raping women – who were then in their turn killed. The methods of slaughtering peasant fisherfolk were disgusting – but then we have to remember that this was a fairly disgusting age. Around this time the Galwegian warriors, on the west of Scotland, were enjoying the sport of impaling babies. The difference between the Vikings and such savages as the Galwegians was that the former had built up for themselves some kind of philosophical construct to account for their actions; their mythology gave them a way whereby they could justify the most bestial behaviour. Their gods dictated that men should be almost inhumanly brave in death, and so it was a token of respect to a defeated foe to give him the maximum latitude to display his bravery. In this respect the Vikings did, though, show a great deal of honesty: should one of their number be submitted to similar tortures it was expected of him that he should bear them without undue complaint, and should bear no grudge into the afterlife against his tormentors. The whole ethical system bears a great resemblance to that of the school playground – except that the bullies (the Vikings) were encouraged rather than discouraged by the teachers (the gods) in their acts of brutality.

TOP RIGHT *Danish Iron Age grave of a woman. The large silver brooch bears a runic inscription; the silver coin near to the necklace is the coin to pay for entry into the afterlife – the Scandinavian equivalent of 'Charon's penny'.*

BOTTOM RIGHT *A fifth-century horned god, gold, from Gallehus, Denmark.*

6

TOP RIGHT *A Danish bronze plaque of a horse dating from about AD 400–800.*

MIDDLE RIGHT *A Norwegian plate, in gold, from the fifth century.*

BOTTOM RIGHT *Twelfth-century gilt panel from Jutland, purporting to show the baptism around 960 of the Viking king, Harald Bluetooth, by Bishop Poppo.*

At first sight it seems that there is very little to recommend the Viking people: their civilization was based on war, looting, aggression, rape and other crimes that make the average modern human being blench. The truth was, though, that these crimes made most of the members of the Viking culture blench, too. They were content that the warriors should travel far afield to terrorize distant lands – after all, if innocents are going to be massacred, your priorities are that you shouldn't be one of them and that the persecution should be happening as far away as possible, so that you have no direct experience of it.

However, even the most warlike of the Vikings did pay lip-service to an ethical system. Most of the tenets of this system bore little resemblance to the modern commandments: in one poem Odin gives advice about how not to be cheated or to do self-evidently stupid things. For our 'Thou shalt not commit adultery', for example, we have Odin's advice that adultery's all right as long as you don't get caught by the jealous spouse and as long as you don't whisper any dangerous secrets into the ear of your lover in a moment of passion.

But however much we may have doubts about this ethical code we have to acknowledge that it was *there*. The contemporaneous Celts seem to have had a much more rigorous scheme of ethical behaviour, but they could be equally cruel. The Christian peoples, whose own mythology affected that of the Vikings, had a far more benign system of ethics yet used it as justification to burn or fry people alive. Greek morality, never too delectable in the first place, was perverted by the Romans into an ethical system so repulsive that words fail us.

And so we return to the Vikings. They lived in lands which were not particularly hospitable to life – the summers were short and the winters long, and always the glaciers in the north seemed threatening. They tried to explain the things they saw around them. The crashing of thunder must

be Thor throwing his mighty hammer, Miölnir, at the frost giants. The cracking of the glaciers must be the cries of the frost giants themselves. The rainbow must surely be a bridge between the land of the gods and the land of the mortals.

It is hard to assess the overall impact of the Vikings on our modern culture; at best it was minimal. However, the mythology which the Norse people have left us – even if in only the most fragmented form – has had a powerful affect on our imaginations. JRR Tolkien's *The Lord of the Rings* owes a great deal to it; then there is Alan Garner's *The Weirdstone of Brisingamen*. Jack Yeovil's long story 'The Ignorant Armies' is based very directly on the legend of Valhalla. My own series of novels, *The Legends of Lone Wolf*, written in conjunction with Joe Dever, draw extensively on the Viking mythology – and, in doing so, are typical of the genre called 'fighting fantasy'. The list of modern fiction based on Norse mythology is long.

In this book I have attempted to tell all of the significant tales. The overall chronology of the mythology is problematical; the details of many of the legends equally so. I have attempted to make the whole system of stories as self-consistent as possible, although I've pointed out instances where the task has proved completely impossible. I am reassured by the fact that every other writer on the subject has found similar difficulties. Viking mythology is not a single continuous story; instead it is a set of stories – many of them very good ones – that relate to each other only with difficulty.

JG

7

ONE

Guide to Gods, Goddesses and Others

Norse mythology is very complex and its surviving sources are not always as clear as they could be. Some people may therefore disagree with the way in which, in this chapter, I have classified the various important figures from the legends; one person's mortal could be another person's god or giant or dwarf.

LEFT *Eighth-century Swedish bronze matrix used for making helmet decorations. The boar's head on the helmet indicates that these warriors were dedicated to the cult of Frey, whose boar was called Hildisvin.*

GODS AND GODDESSES

AEGIR, HLER   The god of the sea. *See* Chapter 3.

BALDER   A beautiful and gentle god, slain inadvertently by his brother Hoder (*q.v.*) as a result of Loki's trickery. *See* Chapter 3.

BOLWERK   One of the pseudonyms used by Odin (*q.v.*) for his adventures among mortals.

BRAGI   The god of music, poetry and eloquence, the son of Odin and Gunnlod (*q.v.*), the giantess whom he had seduced. Bragi married Idun (*q.v.*). Odin carved runes on his tongue and gave him the job of composing songs to honour the gods and the dead heroes in Valhalla.

DELLINGER   (Delling) The god of dawn and the third husband of Night (*q.v.*). Their son was Dag (*q.v.*).

EIRA   (Eyra) One of the attendants of Frigga and also the goddess of medicine. To the Norse the medical deity was naturally female (unlike, for example, the Greek god Asclepius) since by their tradition only women practised medicine.

FJORGYN   (Erda, Jörd) The earth goddess and one of Odin's three wives. She and Odin combined to produce Thor (*q.v.*).

FORSETI   The god of justice and truth, son of Balder and Nanna (*q.q.v.*). As soon as he became known to the other gods of Asgard he was honoured; they gave him the hall Glitnir which had a silver roof supported on pillars of gold. Forseti had the ability to talk so eloquently that foes would make peace; if they didn't, Forseti would strike them dead.

FREY   (Freyr, Fro) One of the Vanir race of gods. The son of Njord (*q.v.*), Frey came to Asgard as a

LEFT *Eleventh-century gravestone from the cemetery at Ed, Uppland, Sweden. The runic inscription begins: 'Thorsten caused this monument to be made in memory of Sven, his father . . .' Of course, this wasn't the Thorsten who featured among the Norse heroes.*

hostage along with his father and his sister Freya (*q.v.*). All three liked it so much there that they stayed. Frey was a fertility god – as, indeed, were the other named Vanir. *See* Chapter 3.

FREYA   (Freyja) The goddess of sex and, later, also of war and death – a curious juxtaposition of responsibilities. One of the Vanir, she came to Asgard as a hostage accompanied by her father Njord and her brother Frey (*q.q.v.*). She married the God Od, who deserted her; thereafter she divided her time between mourning his absence and being promiscuous. In the German version of the Teutonic myth she is identified with Frigga (*q.v.*). *See* Chapter 3.

FRIDLEEF   One of the pseudonyms used by Frey (*q.v.*) for his adventures among mortals.

FRIGGA   (Bertha, Frigg, Holda, Nerthus, Wode) The most important goddess of Asgard; one of the three wives of Odin and the mother of Balder and Hoder (*q.q.v.*). She was the principal goddess of fertility. Ve (*q.v.*) and Vili are reputed to have slept with her, and the same has been said of Ull (*q.v.*). There has been a certain amount of confusion between her and Freya (*q.v.*), to the extent that in the German version of the Teutonic myth the two of them were regarded as the same deity. *See* Chapter 3.

RIGHT *Eighteenth-century illustration of Hermod riding down to Hel on Sleipnir in his attempt to rescue Balder.*

FULLA A goddess who acted as Frigga's attendant and messenger; she was a fertility goddess.

GANGRAD One of the pseudonyms used by Odin (*q.v.*) for his adventures among mortals.

GEFJON (Gefion) A goddess who served as one of Frigga's attendants. She slept with Gylfi (*q.v.*), king of Sweden, and was consequently allowed by him to claim as much of his nation as she could plough within a 24-hour period. She fetched four huge oxen, who were the four sons she had borne to a giant, and within the requisite 24 hours wrenched free a colossal area of Sweden, which her sons towed out to sea. The tract of land is now the island known as Zealand; the hole in Sweden was soon filled up with water, becoming Lake Malaren. We are told by most of the sources that this is an explanation of why Zealand is exactly the same shape as Malaren; unfortunately, a swift check with a map of Scandinavia shows that the two share no resemblance whatsoever, and are of vastly different sizes.

GERSEMI One of Freya's and Od's two daughters.

GNA (Liod) A servant of Frigga (*q.v.*) who acted as the great goddess's messenger. Perhaps her most significant mission was to bring the apple of fertility to the mortal Rerir (*q.v.*).

GRIMNIR One of the pseudonyms used by Odin (*q.v.*) for his adventures among mortals.

HEIMDALL A somewhat puzzling god born from nine giantess mothers simultaneously (*see* Wave Maidens). As Riger he wandered around Midgard impregnating women to found the serf, peasant and warrior races. He was the guardian of the rainbow bridge Bifrost. *See* Chapter 3.

HEL A goddess or a monster, a daughter of Loki and Angrboda (*q.q.v.*), who ruled over Niflheim. Opinions differed over whether she was alive or dead. After the death of

the god Balder she was asked by Hermod if she would simply allow the much-loved god to leave her premises; her response was that she didn't think that Balder was nearly as much-loved as all that. She was similarly unsympathetic when Bragi turned up hoping to recover Idun. Ull, in his role as god of winter, was supposed to spend a couple of months each year as Hel's lover. Some versions of the mythology say that one of the Norns, Skuld, was the same person as Hel. She and her ghostly army will support the other gods at Ragnarok, after which her domain will be consumed by flames.

HERMOD (Irmin) The son of Odin and Frigga (*q.q.v.*). He welcomed the heroes to Valhalla and otherwise acted as the equivalent of the Greek god Hermes. His most spectacular errand was to Hel (*q.v.*) in an effort to recover the god Balder (*q.v.*); *see* Chapter 3.

HLER According to a version of the Creation myth, one of the first gods. *See* Kari.

HLIN A goddess who attended Frigga (*q.v.*). She was the goddess of consolation and very beautiful; she kissed away mourners' tears, relieved grief and heard the prayers of mortals, passing them on to Frigga with recommendations that she answer them.

ABOVE *A pair of dragons depicted on a carved stone from Öland, Sweden.*

HNOSS One of Freya's and Od's two daughters.

HODER (Hod, Hodur) The twin brother of Balder. Because of Loki's trickery, Hoder unwittingly slew Balder and was therefore condemned to death; the justice involved is dubious, to say the very least. In due course Hoder was killed by Vali (*q.v.*), specially bred for the task.

HOENIR (Honir) There are two versions of the story about the earliest gods. In one Odin and his brothers Ve (*q.v.*) and Vili gave to humanity the gifts the species has. The alternative is that Odin's first brothers were Hoenir and Loki (*q.v.*). According to this version Hoenir gave to humanity the gifts of motion and the senses.

IDUN The goddess of spring and of immortal youth. She was the daughter of the dwarf Ivald and the wife of the god Bragi (*q.q.v.*). See Chapter 3.

KARI According to some versions of the Creation myth (*see* Chapter 2) the sons of the giant Ymir (*q.v.*) were Hler (the sea), Kari (the air) and Loki or Lodur (fire). These three gods gave birth to the giants or monsters Beli, Fenris, Grendel, Gymir, Hel, Mimir, Thiassi and Thrym (*q.q.v.*).

KVASIR A somewhat enigmatic figure, in that it is uncertain whether he was a god or merely a supernatural being. If a god, he was probably one of the Vanir, but with an admixture of Aesir. He was brought into existence at the end of the war between the Aesir and the Vanir; as a token of the truce all the gods spat into a ceremonial vase, and from their spittle they generated Kvasir. He became renowned for wisdom and virtue, and was consequently murdered in his sleep by two dwarfs called Fialar and Galar, who wished to take his wisdom for the benefit of the dwarf race. They drained his blood into three containers (a kettle or cauldron called Odhroerir and two bowls called Boden and Son), mixed it with honey and fermented it to produce a brew that had the startl-ing effect, when drunk, of turning the drinker into a poet. We've all come across drinks like this. The murderous pair later disposed of the giant Gilling (*q.v.*) and his wife, and as a consequence were forced by the giant Suttung (*q.v.*) to hand over the mead they had brewed. Suttung's daughter Gunnlod (*q.v.*) was put in charge of guarding the mead, but Odin seduced her and, in her passion, she allowed him to drain all three vessels. As soon as he had done so, Odin turned himself into an eagle and flew back to Asgard. Suttung, realizing at last what had been going on, likewise turned himself into an eagle and flew off in pursuit. Odin just made it to Asgard, where the other gods had laid out all kinds of jars and pots to take the blood of Kvasir, which Odin dutifully vomited up. Some of the mead, however, had been leaked by Odin during his flight to Asgard, which is one of the reasons why the mortals of Midgard could on occasion spout fine poetry. The other reason was that, when in a generous mood, Odin would give a dose of the mead to a mortal.

LODUR According to one version of the Creation myth, Odin's brothers were Hoenir (*q.v.*) and Lodur; these three gave humanity its life. Lodur's contributions were blood and a healthy complexion. Lodur can be equated with Loki (*q.v.*).

LOFN An attendant of Frigga. A beautiful maiden, Lofn had the responsibility for easing the path of true love.

LOKI The 'wizard of lies' and in many ways the most interesting of all the gods of Asgard. Loki was related to Odin, but the exact nature of the relationship is muddled. He came to Asgard either as of right or because Odin entered into a blood-brotherhood with him. *See* Chapter 3; *see also* Thokk (giantess).

MAGNI A son of Thor and the giantess Iarnsaxa (*q.q.v.*). He rescued his father after the latter's duel with the giant Hrungnir (*q.v.*). After

LEFT Tenth-century cross shaft from Sockburn, County Durham, Britain, showing a mounted figure with a bird on his shoulder. This almost certainly represents Odin, only one of his ravens being visible. The figure below may be a valkyrie.

Ragnarok Magni and his brother Modi will possess Thor's hammer Miölnir.

MIMIR The wisest god of all the Aesir; he – or, at least, his head – guarded a spring (Mimir's Well) at the base of Yggdrasil (*q.v.*). There is some confusion concerning his decapitation, but it seems that he and Hoenir were sent by the Aesir to the Vanir as hostages to protect the truce agreed between the two families of gods. The Vanir did not like Hoenir so they killed Mimir – an explanation so illogical that one cannot believe it even of the gods. It is possible that he was the creator of the sword Miming (*q.v.*). Odin made a habit of consulting Mimir's head on occasions when he was stuck for advice; in some versions it is reported that Odin's loss of one eye came about because he had to give it to Mimir's head as down payment for this counselling service.

MODI A son of Thor and the giantess Iarnsaxa (*q.q.v.*). After Ragnarok he and his brother Modi will possess Thor's hammer Miölnir.

NANNA The wife of Balder (*q.v.*).

NERTHUS (Hlodin) The wife of Njord (*q.v.*); a goddess often equated with Frigga (*q.v.*). *See* Chapter 3.

NJORD The father of Frey and Freya; one of the Vanir; a god of the sea who slowly attained ascendance over the Aesir sea-god Aegir (*q.v.*). He was the husband of both the giantess Skadi and the goddess Nerthus (*q.q.v.*).

NORNS The three goddesses concerned with destiny; called Skuld ('Being'), Urd ('Fate') and Verdandi ('Necessity'), they were obviously closely related in concept to the Fates of Greek mythology. They sprinkled Yggdrasil (*q.v.*) with holy water every day so that it would stay in tiptop condition. They were also keen weavers, producing webs of great vastness but haphazard design, as if they didn't know what the outcome of their weaving was likely to be. Two of the sisters, Urd (who was incredibly

old) and Verdandi (who was young and lovely in a sort of rock-jawed way), were generally pretty friendly towards mortals, but Skuld was swift to take offence over the most trivial slight or perceived slight – *see*, for example, the story of Nornagesta (*q.v.*). Skuld also had a habit of ripping up the webs of the three sisters when they were nearly finished.

NOTT The goddess of night; daughter of the giant Norvi (*q.v.*). She had three lovers/husbands: Naglfari (*q.v.*), to whom she bore Aud (*q.v.*); Annar (*q.v.*), who gave her the daughter Erda (*q.v.*); and Dellinger (*q.v.*), whose son by her was called Dag (*q.v.*).

OD (Odur) The first husband of Freya (*q.v.*). She loved him madly but he was a god with a roving heart; he departed in search of mortal bimbos. Freya spent the rest of eternity in a confusing mix of mourning and copulation.

ODIN (Wodan, Woden, Wotan) The son of Börr and Bestla (*q.q.v.*) and the father of Thor, Balder, Hoder, Tyr, Bragi, Heimdall, Ull, Vidar, Hermod and Vali (*q.q.v.*). His wives were Fjorgyn, Frigga and Rind (*q.q.v.*). He was the chief god in the Norse pantheon. One of his frequent habits was to roam around Midgard in human guise seducing and impregnating women; many mortals were therefore able to trace their ancestry back to Odin rather than to travelling sales-men. *See* Chapter 3.

RAN The wife of Aegir (*q.v.*), and like him associated with the sea. She had a net which she used to drag down drowning people. *See* Chapter 3.

RIGER One of the pseudonyms used by Heimdall (*q.v.*) for his adven-tures among mortals.

RIND (Rinda) A goddess men-tioned only as the third wife of Odin, and who gave birth to his son Vali (*q.v.*). She was by all accounts frigid, being the goddess of the frozen soil. There is some confusion between her and the mortal Rind (*q.v.*), daughter of King Billing; it is possible that the two were originally the same character.

SAGA A mistress of Odin whom the god visited for a daily drink at her hall, Sokvabek (*q.v.*).

SATAERE The Teutonic god of agriculture, possibly one of the many personae of Loki (*q.v.*).

SIF The goddess who married Thor and bore his stepson (by Odin) Ull (*q.q.v.*). She was exceptionally proud of her golden hair, so Loki (*q.v.*) cut it all off while she slept. *See* Chapter 3.

SIGYN The third wife of Loki (*q.v.*) and the one who was unremit-tingly faithful to him; she bore his mortal sons Narve and Vali (*q.q.v.*). Even after Loki had been thrown out of Asgard because of his crimes Sigyn remained loyal to him. *See* Chapter 3.

SKULD One of the Norns (*q.v.*).

SNOTRA One of Frigga's attend-ants and also the omniscient goddess of virtue.

SUMMER One of the early gods. He was loved by all except Winter (*q.v.*).

SVASUD A beautiful and gentle god whose son was Summer (*q.v.*).

SYN A goddess who guarded the door of Frigga's palace against un-welcome visitors. Once she had decided to refuse someone entry there was no possibility of changing her mind, and appeals to higher authority were fruitless. She was therefore responsible for all trials and tribunals among mortals.

THOR The son of Odin and Fjorgyn (*q.q.v.*). Thor was associated with thunder, the sky, fertility and the law. Armed with his hammer and his girdle of strength, he had a simple way of righting wrongs: if it moves, kill it. The other gods – notably Loki (*q.v.*) – took advantage of Thor's simplicity on numerous occasions. *See* Chapter 3.

TYR The god of war; son of Frigga by either Odin or the giant Hymir (*q.q.v.*). He was generally regarded as the bravest of all the gods. When the Aesir were preparing to bind Fenris using the chain called Gleipnir (*q.q.v.*), the giant wolf refused to submit unless one of the gods put his arm in the wolf's mouth as a guarantee. Tyr volunteered and thereby lost his right hand.

BELOW *Nineteenth-century book illustration of the chained Loki tended by his faithful wife Sigyn.*

ABOVE *Nineteenth-century book illustration showing Tyr, the bravest of all the gods.*

RIGHT *Nineteenth-century book illustration showing Ull, the god of winter, hunting, archery, death and skiing.*

ULL (Holler, Oller, Uller, Vulder) The god of winter, hunting, archery, death and skiing; a son of Sif, stepson of Thor and maybe husband of the giantess Skadi (*q.v.*). Ull, possibly a lover of Frigga, was regarded as the next most important god after Odin but never attained great popularity because of the frigid season with which he was associated. Some versions of Norse mythology tell how each year, in the summer, Ull is forced to spend some months in Hel so that Odin, in his guise as the god of summer, can govern the weather. The Aurora Borealis was believed to be Ull putting on a visual display.

URD (Urdr, Wurd) One of the Norns (*q.v.*).

VAK One of the pseudonyms used by Odin (*q.v.*) for his adventures among mortals.

VALI The son of Odin and Rind (*q.v.*). This god was conceived deliberately to avenge the death of Balder. He is not to be confused with the Vali who was the son of Loki and Sigyn (*q.q.v.*). *See* Chapter 3.

VALTAM One of the pseudonyms used by Odin (*q.v.*) for his adventures among mortals.

VARA One of Frigga's attendants. Vara was responsible for the keeping of oaths, the punishment of perjurers and rewarding people who kept their word despite any adversity.

VASUD The father of Vindsval and grandfather of Winter (*q.q.v.*). By all accounts Vasud was a very unfriendly god.

VE One of the three sons of Borr and grandsons of the giant Ymir, the other two being Odin and Vili. The three killed their grandfather and out of his body created Midgard, the world of mortals. According to some legends, Odin once spent so long away from Asgard, journeying in the mortal world, that Ve and Vili took over both the throne and Frigga – apparently without any objections on her part.

VECHA One of the pseudonyms used by Odin (*q.v.*) for his adventures among mortals.

VERDANDI One of the Norns (*q.v.*).

VIDAR The son born to Odin and the giantess Grid (*q.v.*). He will slay Fenris (*q.v.*), survive Ragnarok and avenge the death of Odin.

VILI *see* Ve.

VJOFN One of Frigga's attendants. Vjofn's responsibilities to the mortal world focused on conciliation: she strove to keep the peace, bring quarrelling spouses to concord and bend the hardest of hearts to love. Her role seems somewhat paradoxical, given the Vikings' penchant for glorifying warfare.

VÖR One of Frigga's attendants. Her name meant 'faith', and she had full knowledge of the future.

WINTER The vile enemy of the god Summer (*q.v.*); son of Vindsval and grandson of Vasud (*q.q.v.*).

WYRD The mother of the Norns (*q.v.*).

15

GIANTS AND GIANTESSES

ANGRBODA The mother of Loki's hideous children Hel, Jormungand and Fenris (*q.q.v.*).

BAUGI The brother of Suttung (*q.v.*). This giant employed Odin as a labourer when the god was on his way to Suttung's hall intent on stealing the mead of poetry.

BELI One of the descendants of Kari (*q.v.*). The same name was given to the brother of Gerda (*q.v.*) who lost his life in an attack on Frey.

BERGELMIR (Farbauti) The only giant who survived the deluge caused by the blood of the murdered giant Ymir (*q.v.*). According to some versions of Norse mythology, Bergelmir was the father of Loki (*q.v.*), the mother being Laufeia (*q.v.*).

BESTLA The wife of Börr (*q.v.*) and mother of Odin, Ve and Vili (*q.q.v.*).

BOLTHORN The father of Bestla (*q.v.*).

FENIA A giantess who, along with Menia (*q.v.*), was unlucky enough to be enslaved by Frodi, king of Denmark (*q.v.*).

GEIRROD A would-be vanquisher of Thor. Geirrod captured Loki (who was in the guise of a falcon) and forced him to promise to deliver Thor to his hall. *See* Chapter 3.

GERDA A frost giantess of spectacular beauty often associated with the Aurora Borealis; she became the wife of the god Frey (*q.v.*).

GIALP The name of one of the Wave Maidens (*q.v.*) and also of a daughter of Geirrod (*q.v.*).

GILLING A victim of the murderous dwarfs Fialar (*q.v.*) and Galar. Gilling was drowned, but there are different accounts as to how the pair

ABOVE *Nineteenth-century book illustration showing the giantess Gunnlod in the process of being seduced by Odin, whose aim was to gain from her the mead of poetry.*

effected this. One version has it that they came across him sleeping on a riverside and simply rolled him into the water; another says that they sent him fishing in a leaky vessel; a third says that they took him fishing, capsized the boat in the knowledge that he couldn't swim, and rowed home with a merry song on their lips. Gilling's wife was understandably a bit upset by all this, so the dwarfs dropped a millstone on her head, to fatal effect. Gilling's son was Suttung (*q.v.*).

GREIP The name of both a daughter of Geirrod (*q.v.*) and one of the Wave Maidens (*q.v.*); *see also* Gialp.

GRENDEL According to one version of the myths, a sea giant descended from Ymir (*q.v.*). Grendel hit the heights in Old English myth through being slain by the hero Beowulf.

GRID A giantess who gave a night's lodging to Thor and Loki as they travelled towards the hall of the giant Geirrod (*q.v.*). After Loki had fallen asleep, Grid told a drunken Thor that Geirrod was planning to kill him and that he was foolish to make the journey without his hammer and his girdle of strength. She gave him gloves made of iron, a replacement girdle of strength, and an unbreakable staff. On another occasion she seems to have given her son, the god Vidar (*q.v.*; the father was Odin), a massive shoe made out of either leather or iron.

GUNNLOD The daughter of Suttung (*q.v.*), seduced by Odin in order to gain the mead of poetry. The result of their coupling was Bragi (*q.v.*).

GYMIR The father of Gerda (*q.v.*); he has also been equated with the son of Aegir (*q.v.*) and with Aegir himself.

HRAESVELGR A giant whose name means 'corpse-eater'. He sat in the far north in the guise of an eagle; the cold winds from there were the result of him flapping his wings.

HRUNGNIR The strongest of all the giants. He reckoned that his horse Gullfaxi could outrace Odin's steed Sleipnir, and proposed a race. *See* Chapter 3.

HRYM The steersman who will be at the helm of the frost giants' ship when they war with the Aesir during Ragnarok.

BELOW The giant Hymir (on the right) out on a fishing expedition with the god Thor, who is attempting to catch Jormungand, the World Serpent. This is a fragment from the tenth-century cross found at Gosforth, Cumbria, Britain. With a little imagination we can work out that the bait Thor is using is the head of an ox.

HYMIR An elderly giant who was unfortunate enough to own an extremely large cauldron. The god Aegir (*q.v.*) was honest enough to admit to the other Aesir that his own cauldron was not really big enough to brew sufficient quantities of ale for them to get drunk; Thor announced at once that he and Tyr would go and find a cauldron of suitable dimensions. They ended up at the hall of Hymir; the giant was less than delighted by his guests but treated them hospitably, his mask of politeness staying in place even when Thor scoffed two out of the three oxen Hymir had slain in their honour.

The following day Thor behaved very badly even by his own standards. He and Hymir decided to go fishing together; when the giant suggested that Thor should go and find some bait, the god slew Hymir's biggest bull, Himinbrioter, in order to put its head on his hook. Thor then rowed their boat far out to sea and caught the World Serpent, Jormungand (*q.v.*); he was just about to despatch the beast when Hymir, terrified, cut the line. Thor hit the giant with his hammer, knocking him overboard, but Hymir swam to shore and met Thor there amicably. The two of them then breakfasted on a couple of whales Hymir had caught; after the repast the giant challenged the god to smash his beaker. Thor threw the vessel at everything in sight but without success; finally he shattered it by throwing it at Hymir's forehead, the only available substance stronger than the beaker itself.

Hymir then told Thor and Tyr that they could have the cauldron; Tyr was unable to lift it, and even Thor could do so only with difficulty. As the gods were leaving Hymir summoned his fellow frost giants and suggested that a bit of deicide might be fun. They attacked Thor and Tyr, but Thor killed them all with his hammer. (Since Hymir had been courteous and hospitable up to this point we must suspect that the attack on the gods was a later invention, devised solely to give an excuse for the slaughter.) The two gods then triumphantly returned with the cauldron to the hall of Aegir.

HYNDLA   A giant enchantress. Freya's lover Ottar (q.v.) was in dispute with another hero, Angantyr (q.v.), over a piece of property. The Thing (q.v.) had decreed that whichever of the two men could show the more distinguished lineage would win the lawsuit. Freya turned Ottar into the likeness of a boar which she called Hildisvini and rode to Hyndla's dwelling. She persuaded the giantess to trace Ottar's ancestry back for many generations and to give him a draught of a magical brew so that he would remember all the details. Ottar was able to recite his lineage in its entirety. Angantyr was not so assisted and therefore lost the case.

HYRROKIN   A giantess who launched Balder's great funeral boat, *Ringhorn*. She travelled about on a wolf, using serpents for reins.

IARNSAXA   (Jarnsaxa) The name of a mistress of Thor and also of one of the Wave Maidens (q.v.). Magni and Modi (q.q.v.) were Thor's sons by the former.

MENIA   A giantess who, along with Fenia (q.v.), was unlucky enough to be enslaved by Frodi, king of Denmark (q.v.).

MUNDILFARI   The father of Mani and Sol (q.q.v.).

NORVI   (Narvi) The mother of Night (q.v.).

SENJEMAND   A giant who fell in love with a mortal maiden called Juternajesta (q.v.); she rejected him out of hand, on the grounds that he was far too old and repulsive. Senjemand was made a little unhappy by this, and decided to kill her. From a distance of 80 miles he loosed off an arrow at her. The arrow would have killed her had it not been for the intervention of one of Juternajesta's other admirers, the giant Torge, who threw his vast hat in the air to intercept the

missile. Senjemand saddled his horse to flee, fearing that Torge would exact terrible revenge for the attempted murder, but just then the Sun rose and transformed Senjemand, the arrow and the hat into stone.

SKADI   A giantess, daughter of Thiassi. For a time she was married to the god Njord. *See* Chapter 3.

SKRYMIR   A disguise adopted by Utgard-Loki (q.v.).

SKRYMSLI   A giant who defeated a peasant at chess and thereby won the ownership of the peasant's son. The peasant called upon Odin, Hoenir and Loki for assistance, the latter saving the boy's life. *See* Chapter 3.

SURT   (Surtr) A flame giant who guarded the realm called Muspell (q.v.); at Ragnarok he will slay Frey and then set all the world alight.

SUTTUNG   The son of Gilling (q.v.). Suttung discovered that the evil dwarfs Fialar (q.v.) and Galar had murdered both of his parents, and threatened to drown them. To save their lives the dwarfs gave him the mead of poetry, which they had brewed out of honey and the blood of the god Kvasir (q.v.). Suttung was very proud of this coup, and told the world about it. Odin, as a mortal called Bolwerk, callously seduced Suttung's daughter Gunnlod (q.v.) so that she allowed him to drink the mead.

THIASSI   (Thiazi) A giant who kidnapped the goddess Idun (q.v.) and her apples. *See* Chapter 3.

THOKK   (Thok) A giantess who refused to obey the Aesir's command that all living things should weep for the death of Balder (q.v.) so that he might be returned from Hel. The general assumption is that Thokk was actually Loki (q.v.) in disguise.

THRUD   The daughter of Thor and Sif (q.q.v.). The dwarf Alvis (q.v.) sought her hand in marriage, and she was not unwilling to accept his proposal; the rest of the Aesir gave their approval to the marriage. How-

ABOVE *A superb animal head, probably from the bow of a Viking longship, discovered during recent dredging of the River Scheldt, Belgium.*

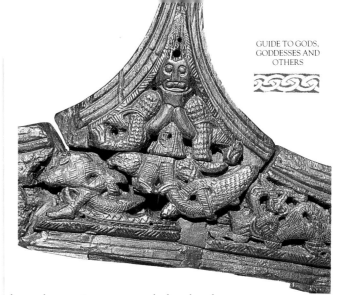

ever, Thor was not so keen. He expressed contempt for the dwarf's diminutive stature and demanded that Alvis prove that, if not a physical giant, he was at least an intellectual one. Thor then hurled tricky questions at the unfortunate dwarf, hour after hour, until the new day broke. Dwarfs were turned to stone by daylight, and this is exactly what happened to the unfortunate Alvis. So much for Thrud's notions of romance.

THRUDGELMIR A six-headed giant born in the dawn of time from the feet of Ymir (*q.v.*); Thrudgelmir in turn produced Bergelmir (*q.v.*).

THRYM Son of Kari (*q.v.*); a giant who stole Thor's hammer and told Loki that it would be returned only on the condition that Freya marry him – for once the goddess declined to offer herself. *See* Chapter 3.

TORGE *see* Senjemand.

UTGARD-LOKI The ruler of Utgard; Thor, Loki, Thialfi and Roskva (*q.q.v.*) went to visit him. *See* Chapter 3.

VAFTHRUDNIR A clever giant who was challenged by Odin (in mortal guise as Gangrad) to a battle of wits; the loser would forfeit his head. Odin answered all the giant's questions correctly, and the giant answered all of Odin's likewise except for the last of them, which was to repeat the words Odin had whispered into the ear of his dead son Balder. The giant immediately realized that no one could answer this question except Odin himself and that the god had tricked him. According to the legend Vafthrudnir announced that the contest had been honourable and willingly surrendered his head.

WADE The father of Völund (*q.v.*), according to Anglo-Saxon and Danish myth.

WAVE MAIDENS There is some confusion about the legend of the nine Wave Maidens – Atla, Augeia, Aurgiafa, Egia, Gialp, Greip, Iarnsaxa, Sindur and Ulfrun – but they seem to have been giantesses and the daughters of the sea-god Aegir. According to one version, Odin was strolling along the shore during one of his frequent sojourns in Midgard when he saw these huge and beautiful women playing in the shallows. The deed followed the impulse, and as a result all nine of them combined to give birth in due course to the god Heimdall (*q.v.*). There is a very similar legend in Irish history. Ruad Rigdonson was sailing from Ireland to Norway with a little fleet of three ships when suddenly all progress ceased. He dived down to see what was happening and found that three giant women were clinging to the rear of each ship. They refused to let him go until he had slept with each of them for a night in their home beneath the sea. He then continued to Norway, promising to stop off for another bout on his way home. However, after seven years in Norway he decided to break his promise and went straight back to Ireland. The furious giantesses pursued him but his ships were too swift, and so in revenge they cut off his child's head and hurled it after him.

It seems certain that these are two different versions of the same tale, with the major difference that in the Irish telling the child is not a god and fails to survive. In addition, the matter of Heimdall's father is uncertain, and various hybrid forms of the legend are to be found.

YMIR (Fornjotnr, Orgelmir) The primaeval giant; *see* Chapter 2.

ABOVE *Detail of the
woodcarving found on
the remains of the
longship used for the
floating funeral pyre at
Oseberg.*

19

DWARFS

Two renditions of the dragon Fafnir being slain by Sigurd: the one BELOW *is a detail from a twelfth- or thirteenth-century wooden portal at Hylestad Church, Setesdal, Norway; the one* OPPOSITE LEFT *is a detail from a tenth-century Viking carving found at Jurby, Isle of Man, Britain.*

ALFRIGG   One of the four dwarfs who manufactured the Brisingamen (*q.v.*) and enjoyed a night of sex with Freya.

ALVIS   Dwarf who was unlucky enough to fall in love with Thor's daughter, the giantess Thrud (*q.v.*).

ANDVARI   A king of the dwarfs whom Loki robbed of all his gold, including a cursed golden ring that brought devastation to the family of Hreidmar (*q.v.*).

AUSTRI   The dwarf who supposedly supported the celestial vault at the east.

BERLING   One of the four dwarfs who manufactured the Brisingamen (*q.v.*) and enjoyed a night of sex with Freya.

BROCK   (Brokk) A dwarf who won a very important bet with Loki. *See* Chapter 3.

DAIN   A dwarf briefly mentioned as a master smith.

DVALIN   One of the four dwarfs who manufactured the Brisingamen (*q.v.*) and enjoyed a night of sex with Freya. He seems also to have been the dwarf whom Loki commissioned to spin the goddess Sif a new head of hair as well as to make the spear, Gungnir, and the collapsible ship, Skidbladnir (*q.q.v.*).

FAFNIR   The son of Hreidmar and the brother of Otter and Regin (*q.q.v.*). Loki killed Otter, and so the three dwarfs determined to kill Odin, Hoenir and Loki. However, Odin told the dwarfs that Loki hadn't realized that Otter was anything other than an animal, and pleaded for their lives. Hreidmar said that the three gods could live if they filled the skin of the dead Otter with gold; Loki was sent off to fetch sufficient quantities of the metal, leaving Odin and Hoenir as hostages.

Loki stole all of the gold belonging to the dwarf Andvari and brought it back to Hreidmar's home; he omitted to mention to the dwarfs that on one piece of it, a ring, there was a curse that would afflict whoever came to be its owner. The gold was sufficient to fill Otter's pelt and even to cover it. Hreidmar said that he was satisfied and so Loki told him about the curse; Hreidmar was not impressed. This

was a mistake on his part, because the curse soon came into operation; Fafnir killed Hreidmar and drove Regin into exile; during this period of exile Regin taught humanity a great deal of technology while Fafnir was transformed into an avaricious dragon. Fafnir was in due coure killed by the hero Sigurd (*q.v.*).

FIALAR (Fjalar) One of the two dwarfs who murdered Kvasir, Gilling (*q.q.v.*) and Gilling's wife.

GALAR One of the two dwarfs who murdered Kvasir, Gilling (*q.q.v.*) and Gilling's wife.

GRERR One of the four dwarfs who manufactured the Brisingamen (*q.v.*) and enjoyed a night of sex with Freya.

HREIDMAR The father of Fafnir (*q.v.*).

IVALD A first-rate blacksmith; the father of Dvalin and of the goddess Idun.

LIT A dwarf murdered by Thor during the cremation of Balder and Nanna.

NABBI A dwarf briefly mentioned as a master smith.

NORDRI The dwarf who supposedly supported the celestial vault at the north.

OTTER A dwarf who took the form of an otter and was slain by Loki; a brother of Fafnir (*q.v.*).

REGIN A brother of Fafnir (*q.v.*). There is some confusion between him and a human called Regin (*q.v.*), who was Sigurd's tutor.

SINDRI (Eitri) The brother of Brock (*q.v.*).

SUDRI The dwarf who supposedly supported the celestial vault at the south.

WESTRI The dwarf who supposedly supported the celestial vault at the west.

ABOVE *Detail from an eighth-century stela at Lillbjärs, Sweden, showing an early version of the Viking longship.*

21

VALKYRIES

ALVIT   One of the three sisters raped by Egil, Slagfinn and Völund (*q.q.v.*). The other two sisters were Olrun and Svanhvit.

BRUNHILD   (Brynhild, Brynhildr) A valkyrie who loved Sigurd (*q.v.*). When he decided to separate from her and be with Gudrun instead, she had him murdered by Guttorm (*q.v.*). Gunnar (*q.v.*), her husband, buried her beside Sigurd. *See* Chapter 4.

GUDRUN   A valkyrie who saw Helgi's prowess in battle and fell in love with him; soon after they were wed. It wasn't long before Helgi (*q.v.*) was murdered by Dag (*q.v.*), and so Gudrun looked around for another husband, eventually settling on the hero Sigurd (*q.v.*). Later she was pressured into marrying Atli (*q.v.*), which she didn't enjoy at all. *See* Chapter 4.

OLRUN   *See* Alvit.

SVANHVIT   *See* Alvit.

SWANHILD   The daughter of Gudrun (*q.v.*). *See* Chapter 4.

OTHER PROPER NAMES

AFI   A mortal whose wife, Amma (*q.v.*), gave birth to Karl (*q.v.*), the progenitor of the race of peasants.

AGNAR   The elder son of Hrauding (*q.v.*). He and his brother Geirrod (*q.v.*), while children, caught the fancy of Odin and Frigga who, disguised as mortals, spent some time with them on an island. When the boys returned home, Geirrod leapt suddenly from their boat and pushed it and Agnar out to sea. Geirrod succeeded to his father's throne. Years later Odin determined to visit King Geirrod as a mortal (taking the name Grimnir) to prove to Frigga that the man was good at heart. Frigga, however, warned Geirrod to look out for

RIGHT *Nineteenth-century book illustration showing Odin being tormented between two fires at the palace of King Geirrod.*

the visiting stranger, telling him that he was an evil sorcerer. Geirrod did not treat Grimnir well: he had him tied up and placed between two fires whose flames lapped at him, roasting him. Agnar, however, had earlier sneaked into his brother's court, working there as a humble servant; he took pity on Grimnir and gave him some ale. Grimnir, revived, sang a prophecy of Geirrod's imminent death by his own sword; then his bonds vanished, the fires went out, and Odin stood before Geirrod in his full glory. Geirrod had drawn his sword to attack the stranger who had uttered such a dire prophecy; when Odin revealed himself the king was so startled that he tripped and fell on the weapon, killing himself. Odin rewarded Agnar with the throne and a promise that prosperity would be his.

Geirrod's son was likewise called Agnar, and this has led to some confusion of the legend. An alternative version is that Agnar the brother survived a harum-scarum ocean voyage after Geirrod had pushed him out to sea, and eked out a bestial existence in a faraway land. It was therefore Agnar the son who took pity on Grimnir and acceded to the throne.

AI A mortal whose wife, Edda (*q.v.*), gave birth to Thrall (*q.v.*) and hence started the race of serfs.

ALFHEIM That part of Asgard (*q.v.*) where the light elves dwelled.

ALSVIDER One of the horses that pulled the chariot conveying the Moon.

ALSVIN One of the horses that pulled the chariot containing the Sun.

AMMA The wife of Afi and the mother of Karl (*q.q.v.*). Nine months after the god Heimdall had stayed a few nights with Afi and Amma she gave birth to a son called Karl (*q.v.*). She thereby became the ancestress of the race of peasants.

ANDHRIMNIR The cook in Valhalla; he spent all his time cooking the boar Saehrimnir to supply dead warriors with food.

ANDVARANAUT The ring of the dwarf Andvari (*q.v.*).

ANGANTYR A hero who lost a case against Ottar (*q.v.*).

ANGURVADEL The magic sword of Viking (*q.v.*).

ANNAR The second husband of Night. He sired her daughter, Earth.

ARVAKR One of the horses that pulled the Sun's chariot across the sky.

ASEGEIR The twelve wise men who decided to unify the Vikings. They set off in a small ship and found themselves blown hither and thither. They made an appeal to the god Forseti (*q.v.*), after which they noticed that there was a thirteenth passenger on board; this person took the helm and steered them towards an island, where he created a spring. A lecture was delivered and then Forseti disappeared. From this time on, the island (Heligoland) was immune from attacks by the Vikings.

ASGARD The home of the Aesir.

ASKR The first man.

ASLAUG The daughter of Sigurd and Brunhild (*q.q.v.*). At the age of three the child was orphaned: Brunhild's father concealed her within a harp. A peasant couple broke open the harp and found the child within; they assumed that she was a mute because she refused to speak. However, she spoke willingly to a passing Viking, Ragnar Lodbrog, and became his wife.

ATLÉ A warrior who challenged Frithiof (*q.v.*).

ATLI A brother of Brunhild (*q.v.*) and king of the Huns; thanks to a magic potion he ended up as the husband of Gudrun (*q.v.*). Gudrun did not like her husband, who was parsimonious to the nth degree; she nevertheless managed to bear two sons by him, Erp and Eitel, both of whom she killed. Atli was responsible for the deaths of both Gunnar and Högni (*q.q.v.*), two of Gudrun's brothers, so it's hardly surprising that the marriage was less than totally happy.

AUD The offspring of Night and her first husband Naglfari (*q.q.v.*).

AUDHUMLA (Audumla) A sacred cow. From the four teats of her udder came four streams of milk that nourished the primaeval giant Ymir (*q.v.*). Ymir was satiated by the milk but then the cow looked around for different sustenance, settling on an iceberg whose salty outer coating she licked away with her rough tongue. The cow kept on licking the iceberg until it melted to leave Buri (*q.v.*), the forefather of the gods.

BALMUNG The sword of Sigmund (*q.v.*), fashioned by Völund (*q.v.*).

BELDEGG A son of Odin who became king of West Saxony.

BELÉ Usurped heir to the throne of the kingdom of Sogn.

BELI The brother of Gerda (*q.v.*). He made the foolish mistake of attacking Frey, the god, lacking his sword, slew him with a nearby antler.

BEYGGVIR (Byggvir) One of Frey's servants. He was Beyla's husband.

BEYLA One of Frey's servants. She was Beyggvir's wife.

BIFROST (Asa-Bridge, Asabru) The bridge linking Midgard to Asgard, guarded by the god Heimdall. Built of fire, air and water, it took the form of the rainbow.

BIL The waning Moon; a sister of Hiuki and companion of Mani (*q.q.v.*). According to some versions, Mani took the two children up from Earth because of their father's cruelty – he'd demanded that they act as water-bearers all night long. There may be some link with Jack and Jill.

BILLING The king of the Ruthenes and father of Rind (*q.v.*).

BILSKIRNIR Thor's palace in Asgard.

BJÖRN A friend and confidant of Frithiof (*q.v.*).

BLODUGHOFI Frey's horse.

BODEN One of the bowls into which the dwarfs Fialar (*q.v.*) and Galar drained the blood of the god Kvasir, whom they had murdered.

ABOVE *Patterns of stones at Lindholm Løje, Denmark, trace out the shapes of longships, commemorating Viking burials there.*

BODVILD Daughter of the king of Sweden, Nidud (*q.v.*). Nidud took Völund (*q.v.*) prisoner, hamstrung him and stole all his property. *See* Chapter 5.

BORGHILD A princess by whom Sigmund (*q.v.*) had two sons, Hamond and Helgi. Sinfiotli (*q.v.*), Sigmund's son by Signy (*q.v.*), killed Borghild's brother in a brawl and so Borghild poisoned him. After Sinfiotli's death Sigmund realized that there was something amiss in the marriage and so divorced her.

BÖRR (Bor) The son of Buri (*q.v.*) and the father of the gods Odin, Ve and Vili.

BRANSTOCK An oak tree that stood in the centre of the hall of Volsung (*q.v.*). At the wedding feast of Siggeir and Volsung's daughter Signy (*q.q.v.*) a stranger suddenly appeared and thrust a sword into the Branstock; whoever could pull the sword out could have it, the stranger said, and it would bring him victory in every battle. Siggeir had a try, but without success, and Volsung's nine eldest sons likewise failed miserably. It was left to the youngest son, Sigmund (*q.v.*), to do the deed. It was because of Siggeir's jealousy about this that the feud sprang up between him and the line of Volsung.

BREIDABLIK Balder's hall in Asgard.

BRIMER (Brimir, Okolnir, Okolnur) One of the halls that will exist after Ragnarok. Here the giants will at last be able to enjoy warmth, for there will be no such thing as cold. Even if there were, the giants wouldn't mind because one of the other delights of Brimer will be endless supplies of strong drink.

BRISINGAMEN An ornament, generally assumed to be a necklace, manufactured by the four dwarfs Alfrigg, Berling, Dvalin and Grerr. Freya came across the smithy of the four while wandering in Svartalfheim and instantly lusted to possess the Brisingamen; the dwarfs instantly lusted after her, and soon a contract was agreed whereby she could have the ornament in return for spending a night of passion with each of them. Loki told Odin, who commanded him to take the necklace away from Freya. In order to regain it Freya, hitherto only the goddess of sex, had to take on the additional portfolios of war and death.

BROCKEN (Blocksberg) The highest peak of the Harz mountains in East Germany. Here the witch-followers of Freya danced on Walpurgisnacht.

BURI The forefather of the gods, brought into existence when the sacred cow Audhumla (*q.v.*) licked an iceberg.

DAG Day; son of Nott by her third husband Dellinger (*q.q.v.*). He travelled daily across the sky, his chariot pulled by the horse Skinfaxi, whose shining mane lit up the world.

DAG The sole survivor of the family of Hunding (*q.v.*) after they had made the foolish mistake of doing battle with Sigmund's sons Sinfiotli and Helgi (*q.q.v.*). Dag bought his life by promising not to avenge the death of his kin, but he betrayed the oath and murdered Helgi.

BELOW *The Lindisfarne Stone, from Northumbria, Britain, showing seven warriors usually thought to be Vikings. It is generally believed that the carving commemorates the first Viking attack on the Holy Island around* AD 793.

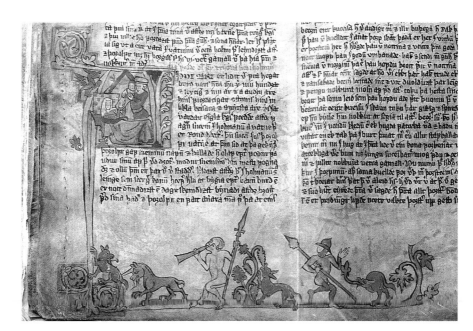

LEFT & RIGHT *A detail from an Icelandic manuscript copy of the* Flateyjarbok, *part of the* Poetic Edda.

DAIN One of the four stags dwelling on Yggdrasil.

DRAUPNIR A gold ring owned by Odin. Every ninth night it spawned eight exactly similar rings.

DROMA The second chain produced by the gods in their attempts to bind Fenris.

DUNEYR One of the four stags dwelling on Yggdrasil.

DURATHOR One of the four stags dwelling on Yggdrasil.

DVALIN One of the four stags dwelling on Yggdrasil. Also the name of a dwarf (*q.v.*).

EARTH The daughter of Norvi; her father was Annar (*q.q.v.*).

ECKHARDT A bosom friend of Tannhäuser (*q.v.*).

EDDA A mortal, the mother of Thrall (*q.v.*) and the ancestress of the race of serfs. The god Heimdall stayed a few nights with Edda and her husband Ai, and nine months later Thrall was born.

EDDAS Two anthologies of Norse legends, the Prose Edda and the Poetic Edda, of which the more important is the former. The Prose Edda was compiled by the Icelandic writer Snorri Sturluson (1178-1241). It is in four parts: a Prologue, 'The Deluding of Gylfi' (*q.v.*), 'Poetic Diction' and 'List of Metres'. The Poetic Edda was compiled about 1270 – i.e., some while later – and is often confusingly called the Elder Edda.

EGIL A brother of Völund (*q.v.*).

EGLIMI King of the Orkney Islands and the father of Hiordis (*q.v.*), the last wife of Sigmund (*q.v.*).

EINHERIAR (Einherjar) The slain warriors who were brought to Valhalla (*q.v.*), there to battle during the day and feast the night away. They will continue this curiously masochistic practice until Ragnarok.

EINMYRIA One of Loki's two daughters by Glut (*q.v.*).

EISA One of Loki's two daughters by Glut (*q.v.*).

EITEL A son of Atli and Gudrun (*q.q.v.*).

ELDE (Eldir) A servant to the god Aegir (*q.v.*).

ELDHRIMNIR The cauldron in Valhalla in which the boar Saehrimnir (*q.v.*) was cooked daily.

ELF (Elb, Helferich, Helfrat) A water sprite whose name was given to

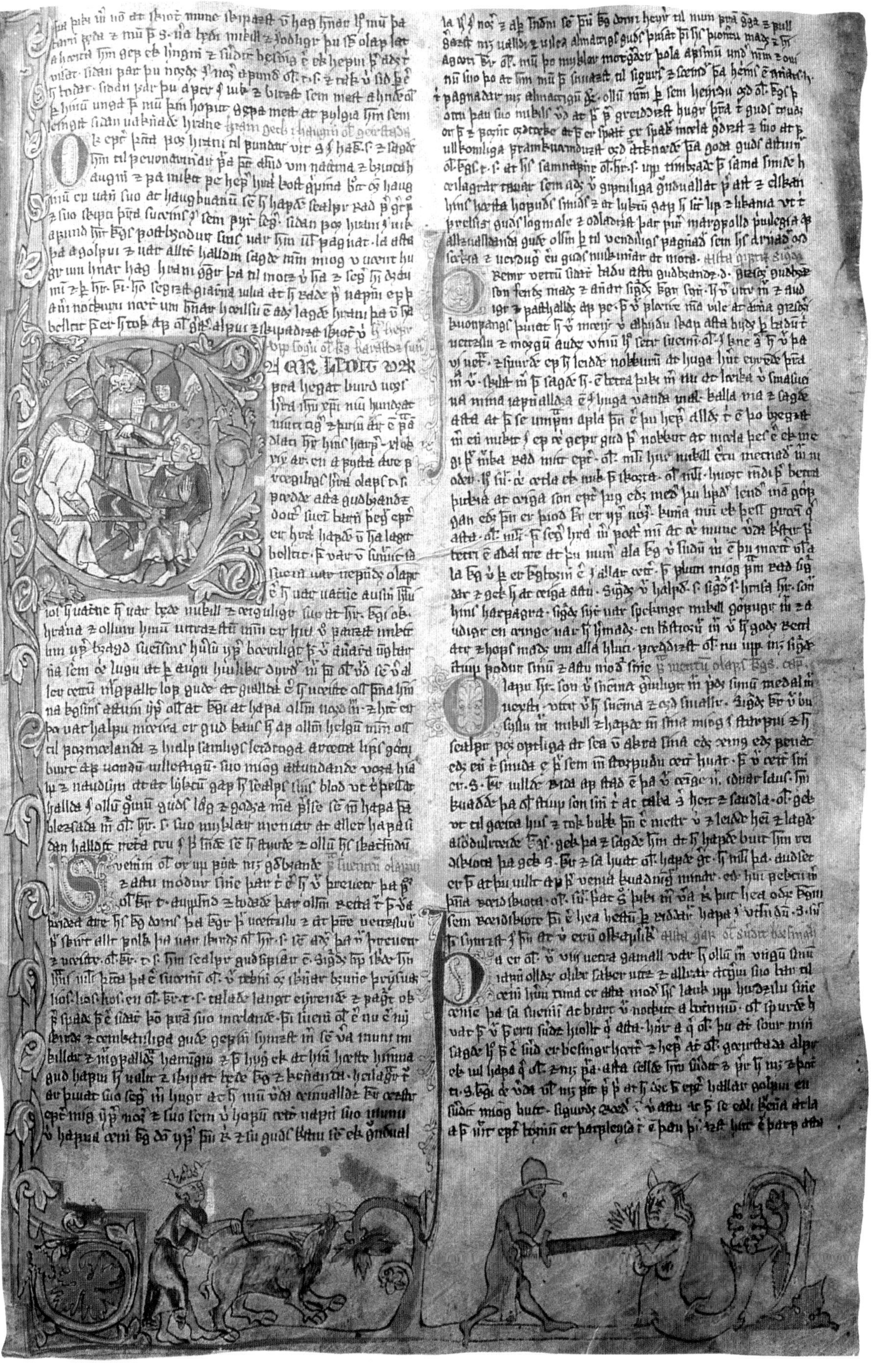

the Elbe River; in certain Teutonic mythologies Elf is regarded as a god. Also, a Viking who married Hiordis after the death of Sigmund and became the stepfather of Sigurd (*q.q.v.*).

ELLI The name of the old woman with whom the god Thor unsuccessfully wrestled during his excursion to Utgard (*q.v.*). Afterwards the giant Utgard-Loki (*q.v.*) explained that Thor hadn't had a chance since Elli was really old age, who can be resisted by no mortal.

ELLIDA The magical dragon ship given by the god Aegir to Viking (*q.q.v.*).

ELVIDNER The hall of the goddess Hel (*q.v.*).

EMBLA The first woman; the sons of Borr created her from an elm tree.

ERMENRICH King of Gothland, a mortal who married the Valkyrie Swanhild (*q.v.*).

ERNA The wife of Jarl (*q.v.*).

ERP A son of Atli and Gudrun (*q.q.v.*).

ESBERN SNARE A lover of Helva (*q.v.*). He wanted to marry Helva and consequently struck a bargain with a troll to the effect that, as soon as the troll had built a church, Esbern should either name the builder or lose his eyes and heart. Luckily Helva helped, naming the troll as 'Fine' (*q.v.*).

FADIR (Fathir) Husband of Modir (*q.v.*), the ancestress of the warrior race.

FAFNIR (dragon) *see under* DWARFS.

FENRIS (Fenrir) Son of the god Loki and the giantess Angrboda (*q.v.*). This child took the form of an enormous wolf and became steadily more threatening to the gods. They tried to fetter the beast using the chains Laeding, Droma and (with success) Gleipnir. *See* Chapter 3.

FENSALIR Frigga's hall in Asgard.

FIMBULVETR (Fimbul-Winter) The three-year winter that will be inflicted upon the world immediately before Ragnarok.

FINE The troll who hoped to slaughter Esbern Snare (*q.v.*).

FIOLNIR (Fjolnir) The son of Frey and Gerda (*q.q.v.*).

FOLKVANG Freya's hall in Asgard.

FREKI One of the two wolves owned by the god Odin.

FREYGERDA A mortal woman who married the god Frey (*q.v.*) in his guise as Fridleef after he had rescued her from the attentions of a dragon. She bore their son Frodi (*q.v.*).

FRITHIOF A Norse hero, son of Thorsten and Ingeborg (*q.q.v.*). *See* Chapter 5.

28

FRODI The son of the god Frey and the mortal Freygerda (*q.q.v.*); he is recorded in Norse mythology as a pacifist king of Denmark who ruled about the time of Christ.

FUNFENG One of the two main servants of the god Aegir; the other was Elde (*q.v.*).

GAMBANTEIN Hermod's magical wand.

GARM A dog at the gate of Hel, chained in the cave Gnipa. When Ragnarok occurs this dog and the god Tyr (*q.v.*) will battle to their mutual death.

GELGIA The end of the chain with which the Aesir finally succeeded in tethering Fenris (*q.v.*).

GERI One of the wolves that accompanied Odin.

GIALLAR The bridge over the Giöll River (*q.v.*). Guarded by Modgud (*q.v.*), this represented the boundary between the mortal world and Niflheim (*q.v.*).

GIALLAR-HORN (Gjall) The trumpet possessed by the god Heimdall (*q.v.*).

GIMLI The hall which, after Ragnarok, will be populated by the surviving gods.

GINNUNGAGAP The primaeval abyss between Muspell and Niflheim (*q.q.v.*). According to the legends, this abyss was so deep that no mortal eye could see to its bottom.

GIOLL The rock to which the Aesir bound Fenris (*q.v.*).

GIÖLL RIVER The boundary of Niflheim (*q.v.*).

GIUKI King of the Nibelungs, husband of Queen Grimhild and father of Gunnar, Guttorm and Hogni (sons) and Gudrun (daughter); the last married Sigurd (*q.v.*).

GLADSHEIM A hall where the Aesir met in council.

GLAUMVOR Second wife of Gunnar (*q.v.*).

GLEIPNIR The third chain used by the Aesir in their attempts to fetter Fenris (*q.v.*).

GLEN The husband of Sol (*q.v.*).

GLITNIR The hall of the god Forseti (*q.v.*) in Asgard.

GLUT The first wife of Loki and mother of Einmyria and Eisa (*q.q.v.*).

GNIPA (Gnippahellir) A cave by the entrance to Niflheim (*q.v.*) in which the dog Garm (*q.v.*) dwelled.

GREYFELL (Grane) The horse belonging to Sigurd (*q.v.*).

GRIMHILD Queen of the Nibelungs, husband of Guiki, and a devious sorceress. It was thanks to her machinations that Sigurd married Gudrun (*q.q.v.*) bigamously and Gunnar married Brunhild (*q.v.*) equally bigamously.

GRIPIR The stable master to Elf (*q.v.*). He gave a prophecy to Sigurd (*q.v.*) of the hero's major future life events and death.

GROA *See* Orvandil.

LEFT *Details of the stern of the Oseberg longship.*

GUDRUN The name of both a Valkyrie (q.v.) and of a mortal (daughter of Giuki and Grimhild – q.q.v.) who was married successively to Sigurd (bigamously, through no fault of her own; their daughter was Swanhild) and Atli (q.q.v.). See Chapter 4.

GULL-TOP Horse belonging to the god Heimdall (q.v.).

GULLFAXI Horse belonging to the giant Hrungnir (q.v.). The animal was given by Thor to his son Magni (q.v.), who freed the god after he had been crushed to the ground by Hrungnir's corpse.

GULLINBURSTI A vast boar made by the dwarfs Brock and Sindri (q.q.v.). The beast eventually became the property of the god Frey.

GULLINKAMBI A cock living in Valhalla, where its crow awakened the Einherjar each morning so that they could resume their battling. The cock will also crow to forewarn the Aesir of the onset of Ragnarok.

GUNGNIR A magical spear commissioned by Loki from the dwarf Dvalin (q.v.) as a present to placate Thor and Sif.

GUNGTHIOF Brother of Hunthiof and son of Frithiof (q.q.v.).

GUNNAR (Gundicarius) Eldest son of Giuki and Grimhild (q.q.v.); he became the husband of the Valkyrie Brunhild (q.v.) through his mother's sorcery.

GUTTORM A son of Giuki and Grimhild (q.q.v.) who was the unhappy recipient of one of his mother's magic potions and consequently killed Sigurd (q.v.) and the latter's baby by Gudrun (q.v.). In his dying seconds Sigurd slew Guttorm.

GYLFI A king of Sweden who permitted Odin to build a city in his country. In another story Gylfi disguised himself as a wayfarer, Gangleri, and journeyed to Odin's hall in Asgard. There he conversed with three mysterious creatures – Har, Iafnhar and Thridi – who described to him the fundamentals of Norse mythology in considerable detail.

HAGAL The foster-father of Sigmund's son Helgi (q.v.).

HAKON The father of Thora (q.v.).

HALFDAN Son of Belé and a close friend of Viking (q.q.v.).

HAM One of two witches (the other was called Heid) summoned up by Helgé to interfere with a voyage of Frithiof (q.q.v.). Frithiof cut up his golden armlet and gave an equal portion to each of his crew so that they would have something with which to propitiate the goddess Ran (q.v.); then he was able to control his ship, Ellida, sufficiently to make mincemeat out of the two witches and the whale upon which they were riding the seas.

HAMDIR A son of Gudrun (q.v.) by her third husband, Jonakur.

ABOVE *Detail of an early-twelfth-century wallhanging in Baldishol Stave Church, Norway, showing a Viking warrior on horseback. The resemblance between this image and that of a Norman – like William the Conqueror – is no coincidence: the name 'Norman' is a version of 'Norsemen', indicating where these conquerors of Normandy originated.*

HAMOND A son of Sigmund and Borghild (*q.q.v.*).

HAR One of the three mysterious beings seen by Gylfi (*q.v.*) at the gate of Odin's hall.

HATI One of the wolves – the other was Sköll (*q.v.*) – that pursued the Sun and Moon across the sky. The name means 'hatred'. Just before Ragnarok Hati will finally succeed in devouring the Moon.

HÁVAMÁL (High Song) A long poem by Odin in which the god set out a code of practice for the Norse.

HEID *See* Ham.

HEIDRUN The goat in Valhalla that produced an endless supply of mead for the dead heroes.

HEIME The son of Völund (*q.v.*) and owner of the sword Miming, made for him by his father.

HEL The realm of the dead in Niflheim (*q.v.*). Either it took its name from the goddess Hel (*q.v.*) or she was named after it when presiding over it. There are many tales of individuals sojourning in Hel, the most notable being the god Balder (*q.v.*); readers are referred to the index.

HELGÉ One of the sons of Belé (*q.v.*); the other was Halfdan (*q.v.*). He refused to let his sister Ingeborg marry Frithiof (*q.v.*) but eventually allowed her to be betrothed to Sigurd Ring (*q.v.*).

HELGI A son of Sigmund and Borghild (*q.q.v.*). He was fostered out to Hagal (*q.v.*); he became a lover of the Valkyrie Gudrun (*q.v.*) but was then slain by the treacherous Hunding Dag (*q.v.*).

HERVOR A daughter of Angantyr (*q.v.*). She raised him from the dead in order to recover the sword Tyrfing (*q.v.*).

HIALLI An unfortunate murdered in place of Högni (*q.v.*).

HILDING The foster-father of Frithiof and Ingeborg (*q.q.v.*).

HIMINBIORG (Himinbjorg) The hall in Asgard of the god Heimdall (*q.v.*).

HIMINBRIOTER (Himinhrjot) A huge ox owned by the giant Hymir (*q.v.*). Thor killed it and used its head as fishbait.

HIORDIS Daughter of Eglimi and, in his later years, a wife of Sigmund (*q.v.*). Lygni (*q.v.*) was so upset that Sigmund's suit should be preferred to his own that he raised an army to take revenge.

HIUKI The waxing Moon; the brother of Bil (*q.v.*) and companion of Mani (*q.v.*).

HLESEY The island near to which the gods Aegir and Ran (*q.q.v.*) lived. The name comes from Aegir's alternative name Hler.

HLIDSKIALF The high throne of Odin from which he could see all over the nine worlds.

RIGHT *Bronze metalwork from a Swedish Viking grave, possibly from the tenth century, apparently showing Thor fishing for Jormungand, the World Serpent.*

HLORA A foster-parent of Thor, whose other foster-parent was Vingnir. Together, Vingnir and Hlora constituted sheet lightning. The god was grateful enough to them both to use as his own alternative names Hlorridi and Vingthor.

HNOSS A daughter of Freya and Od; their other daughter was Gersemi (*q.v.*).

HOFVARPNIR The horse of the goddess Gna (*q.v.*).

HÖGNI A son of Giuki and Grimhild (*q.q.v.*). He and his brother Gunnar (*q.v.*) were the only two to know where the Nibelung hoard had been hidden. When Atli (*q.v.*) tortured Gunnar to find out its location, the latter refused to tell him until he was brought the heart of Högni, saying that he had sworn to keep the information secret so long as his brother was alive. Atli's soldiers brought the heart of a ne'er-do-well, Hialli, pretending that it was Högni's, but Gunnar saw that the heart trembled at his gaze and refused to believe that it was his brother's. So next time the soldiers brought the real thing, which, believe it or not, Gunnar recognized for what it was. Gunnar then told Atli that, since his brother was now dead, only he, Gunnar, knew where the treasure was hidden, and he wasn't telling. So Atli had him thrown into a pit full of venomous serpents, one of which (in some versions said to be Atli's mother in disguise) ended his life.

HRAUDING The father of the youths Agnar and Geirrod (*q.q.v.*) to whom Odin and Frigga took a fancy.

HRIMFAXI The horse of Nott (*q.v.*).

HUGI The boy against whom Thialfi (*q.v.*) was matched in races when Thor was visiting the giant Utgard-Loki (*q.v.*). Hugi won by miles. Later the giant confessed to Thor and his companions that Hugi was actually 'thought' in disguise; Thialfi had lost the races because, of course, nothing physical can run as fast as thought.

HUGIN One of Odin's ravens; the other was Munin.

HUNDING A noble who was infuriated by the impertinence of Helgi (*q.v.*) and consequently waged war against him.

HUNTHIOF Brother of Gungthiof and son of Frithiof (*q.q.v.*).

HUNVOR A Swedish princess rescued and married by Viking (*q.v.*).

HVERGELMIR The cauldron in Niflheim next to which there was one of the roots of Yggdrasil (*q.v.*).

IAFN-HAR One of the three mysterious beings with whom Gylfi (*q.v.*) had a discussion.

IARN-GREIPER The glove belonging to the god Thor.

IDAVOLD (Idavoll) A plain in Asgard.

IFING The river running around the edge of Idavold (*q.v.*).

INGEBORG A daughter of Belé (*q.v.*) whom Frithiof (*q.v.*) married. The same name was given to a wife of Halfdan and a wife of Thorsten (*q.q.v.*).

JARL Like Thrall and Karl (*q.q.v.*) before him, Jarl was the offspring born of one of Heimdall's illicit unions, this time with Modir (*q.v.*); he became the ancestor of the warrior race.

JORMUNGAND (Iörmungandr, Midgardsormr, World Serpent) The serpent who was the child of the god Loki and the goddess Angrbodr. This snake surrounds Midgard, biting on its own tail to complete the circle.

JOTUNHEIM The land of the giants.

JUTERNAJESTA A beautiful girl with whom the giant Senjemand (*q.v.*) fell in love.

KARL The son of an illicit union between the god Heimdall and the mortal Amma (*q.q.v.*); the progenitor, with his wife Snor, of the race of peasants.

KNEFRUD (Wingi) A servant of Atli (*q.v.*) who was supposed to kill the Nibelungs.

KONUR The first king of Denmark, direct descendant of Jarl (*q.v.*).

LAEDING The first chain that the gods produced in their attempts to bind Fenris.

LANDVIDI The hall of the god Vidar (*q.v.*).

LAUFEIA (Nal) The putative mother of the god Loki (*q.v.*).

LEIPTER One of the icy rivers that flowed away from the cauldron Hvergelmir (*q.v.*). On the banks of this river oaths were sworn.

LERAD (Laerad) The uppe branch of Yggdrasil (*q.v.*); alternatively, another name for the great tree itself.

LIF The man who'll survive Ragnarok and father humanity thereafter. His wife will be Lifthrasir.

LIFTHRASIR The woman who'll survive Ragnarok and mother humanity thereafter. Her husband will be Lif. It's interesting that, in the science fiction of the 1950s and 1960s, there were countless tales about the last two survivors of nuclear war (or some other genocidal event) who were by astonishing coincidence always called Adam and Eve, and who would always be able to procreate to produce our successors. Clearly the idea that there's some great catastrophe up ahead, and that humanity as a whole will be saved because of a pair of survivors, is very deeply ingrained in our collective subconscious.

LOGI (Fire) The cook in the hall of the giant Utgard-Loki (*q.v.*). He was entered in an eating race with the god Loki and won by a long way. Later Utgard-Loki confessed that Logi was in reality fire, which devours things more swiftly than any mortal can.

LORELEI A lovely young woman

BELOW Bronze and gilt brooch found in a Viking grave in Norway.

seated upon the St Goar Rock on the Rhine River. She sang a sweet song that enchanted many a mariner to his death.

LORRIDE   One of the daughters of Thor.

LYGNI   A king who wanted to marry Hiordis (*q.v.*) but was rejected by her in favour of Sigmund (*q.v.*); he therefore raised an army and fought a battle with Sigmund's supporters in which the hero was slain.

MAELSTROM   The primaeval whirlpool.

MANAGARM   A wolf who was the child of Iarnsaxa; the father was Fenris (*q.q.v.*).

MANI   The Moon.

MANNIGFUAL   A vast ship owned by the giants, according to a Frisian tradition. Its size can be assessed from the fact that youths instructed to scale the masts were old men by the time they returned!

MEGINGIÖRD   The belt of Thor.

MIDGARD   (Manaheim) The world inhabited by human beings.

MIMING   A sword made by Völund (*q.v.*) for his son Heime; an alternative version is that it was made by the god Mimir (*q.v.*).

MIÖLNIR   The hammer belonging to Thor (*q.v.*). It was forged by the dwarfs Brock and Sindri (*q.q.v.*).

MODGUD   A grim, skeletal woman who guarded the bridge over the river Giöll (*q.v.*).

MODIR   (Mothir) The wife of Fadir and, thanks to a visit from Heimdall, the mother of Jarl (*q.q.v.*). Modir was therefore the progenitor of the warrior race.

MOKERKIALFI   (Mist Calf, Mokkurkalfi) A mock giant made out of clay by the giant Hrungnir (*q.v.*) to battle with Thialfi (*q.v.*).

MUNIN   One of Odin's ravens; the other was Hugin.

LEFT *A dress fastener dating from the Viking period. It is bronze and gilt.*

MUSPELL   The realm of fire, involved in the Creation (*see* Chapter 2). At Ragnarok the giant occupants of Muspell will emerge, led by the realm's guardian, Surt (*q.v.*), to do battle with the gods.

MYSINGER   The Viking leader responsible for murdering Frodi (*q.v.*).

NAGLFARI   The first husband of Night (*q.v.*); their child was Aud (*q.v.*).

NARVE   (Narvi) The mother of Night (*q.v.*).

NASTROND   The part of the realm of Hel (*q.v.*) in which stood the hall to which the wicked went after death. Here the dragon Nidhug (*q.v.*) chewed up their corpses.

NIDHUG   A voracious dragon that chewed up the corpses of evil-doers after their death as well as (presumably for roughage) gnawing at the roots of Yggdrasil.

NIDUD   A king of Sweden who came across Völund (*q.v.*) while the latter was sleeping, took him prisoner, stole all his property, then hamstrung him and set him to work in a smithy forging weapons and ornaments. *See* Chapter 5.

NIFLHEIM   A land of darkness and freezing mist in which lay one of Yggdrasil's roots as well as the region of Hel.

NIGHT   (Nott) The daughter of the giant Norvi. She had three husbands: Naglfari, Annar and Delling.

NINE WORLDS   The worlds that constituted the whole of creation. It is hard to produce a definitive list of them, because of confusion in the legends. Muspell is mentioned in the Prose Edda as the first of all the worlds, yet cannot easily be fitted into the Norse cosmogony. Hel can be considered either as a world or (probably more correctly) as a part of Niflheim – or even, come to that, as just another name for Niflheim!

The worlds existed on three levels, down through all of which Yggdrasil (*q.v.*) penetrated and in each of which it had a root. The bottom-most level contained Hel and Niflheim (or Hel/Niflheim); the middle level contained Jotunheim (the land of giants), Midgard (the middle world or land of mortals), Nidavellir (the land of dwarfs) and Svartalfheim (land of dark elves); the top level contained Alfheim (land of light elves), Vanaheim (land of the Vanir) and, in utmost splendour, Asgard, the home of the gods.

NIP   The father of the goddess Nanna (*q.v.*).

NJORFE   A foe and then bosom friend of Viking and Halfdan (*q.q.v.*). His sons and Viking's sons were less keen on the paternal friendship. *See* Chapter 5.

NÖATÛN   The hall of the god Njord (*q.v.*).

NORNAGESTA   A bard who possessed the gift of youth. This was because, at his birth, someone insulted Skuld (*q.v.*), one of the Norns; she furiously said that the babe would live only as long as it took for a bedside candle to burn down. There was a deal of mourning until one of the other Norns had the wit simply to put the candle out. Nornagesta carried it with him

wherever he went. At the age of 300 he was forced to become a Christian by Olaf Tryggvesson and, to prove that the conversion was not just lip-service, to light the candle-stub. This he did and, when it burnt out, he dropped down dead.

The legend is slightly curious, because it must have originated some time after the Norse had become Christians; yet its clear moral is that people should stick to the old, heathen

RIGHT *Part of a belt-buckle found in a sixth-century chief's grave at Aker, Norway. The work was done in silver and gilt together with niello, gold and garnets.*

religion. Maybe it came into existence as a rumour spread by the die-hards who resented the coming of the new religion?

OD-HROERIR   One of the containers into which the dwarfs Fialar and Galar drained the blood of Kvasir (*q.q.v.*).

ORVANDIL   (Aurvandil) Either the son or the husband of Groa (*q.v.*), the sorceress summoned by Thor to try to get the whetstone out of his head after his duel with the giant Hrungnir (*q.v.*). Groa had assumed that her son/husband was long-dead, but as she chanted her spells to loosen the stone from Thor's forehead the god became so pleased with her that he decided to cheer her up by telling her that her loved one was very much alive, thanks to the good actions of none other than himself, Thor. The god had gone to the land of the frost giants to recover Orvandil, putting him in a basket to carry him home. Unfortunately Orvandil had persisted in sticking a toe out through the wicker of the basket, and this toe had frozen solid; Thor had therefore snapped it off and thrown it up into the sky, where it became a star. Thor took Groa to show her the star as proof of his tale, and she was so excited that she forgot where she had got to in her spells. She lost a job but, we assume, regained her son/husband; Thor was left with a stone embedded in his forehead.

RIGHT Sigurd slays his tutor Regin – a carving from Starkirba Church, Norway. Or was it his tutor? There was also a dwarfish Regin, a brother of Otter, and the coincidence of names has caused some confusion in the legends.

OTTAR A hero who disputed a piece of property with Angantyr. Ottar was lucky enough to get assistance from Freya, and so won the legal argument. For more details, *see* the entry on the giantess Hyndla.

RAGNAR LODBROG Son-in-law of Brunhild and Sigurd through his marriage to their daughter Aslaug (*q.q.v.*).

RAGNAROK The final battle during which the gods will succumb to the forces of evil. *See* Chapter 6.

RANDWER The son of Ermenrich (*q.v.*). He was falsely accused of making love with Swanhild (*q.v.*), and so his father condemned them both to death.

RATATOSK A loquacious squirrel living in Yggdrasil (*q.v.*). Ratatosk spent all its time rushing up and down to relay to the eagle at the top of the tree and the dragon Nidhug (*q.v.*) at its bottom to tell them both the latest insult each had uttered about the other. This squirrel, the object of contempt among the Norse, was obviously the precursor of tabloid journalism.

RATI An auger owned by Odin (*q.v.*).

36

REGIN A very wise man who was appointed by Elf (*q.v.*) to be the tutor of Sigurd (*q.v.*). There is some confusion between this Regin and one of the brothers of the dwarf Fafnir (*q.v.*); often the two are conflated.

RERIR The son and heir of Sigi (*q.v.*). Rerir and his wife were not blessed with a son to inherit the throne until Frigga decided to have compassion on them. She sent her messenger, the goddess Gna, to Rerir with a magic apple which he shared with his wife. Perhaps it was the vitamin C, but nine months later Volsung (*q.v.*) was born to them. They died while the boy was still an infant.

RIND The daughter of King Billing. Odin attempted to seduce her, and later described her in contemptuous terms because she had declined the offer. There is some confusion between her and the goddess Rind (*q.v.*) who became Odin's mistress and gave birth to the god Vali (*q.v.*).

RING A son of Viking (*q.v.*).

RINGHORN The longship on which the god Balder and his wife Nanna (*q.q.v.*) were cremated.

ROSKVA The sister of Thialfi (*q.v.*) and, like him, forced to become a servant of Thor.

ROSSTHIOF A Finnish magician who used his magic to pull travellers into his realm so that he could kill them and take all their treasure. He was also able to read the future, but didn't like doing so. He was captured by Hermod (*q.v.*) and forced to predict that a son of Odin would be murdered but avenged by another son of Odin; these sons were, respectively, Balder and Vali (*q.q.v.*).

SAEHRIMNIR A boar slain daily by the cook Andhrimnir (*q.v.*) and boiled in the cauldron Eldhrimnir to feed the dead warriors in Valhalla; no matter how much they stuffed themselves, the meat of the boar was always sufficient – and the beast returned to life in time to be slaughtered again the next morning.

SAEMING A son of Odin who became a king.

SESSRYMNIR The hall of the goddess Freya (*q.v.*).

SIBICH A dishonest man who told Ermenrich (*q.v.*) that his son Randwer (*q.v.*) had been making love with Swanhild (*q.v.*). The accusation was false but nevertheless Ermenrich had Swanhild and Randwer put to death.

SIEGFRIED *see* Sigurd.

SIGGEIR King of the Goths and Volsungs and cuckolded husband of Signy (*q.v.*). He made the mistake of getting Sigmund and Sinfiotli (*q.q.v.*) angry, and paid with his life.

SIGI Emperor of the Huns and father of Rerir (*q.v.*). Sigi, a son of Odin, seems to have been a rather nasty piece of work, murdering a hunting companion for having killed more game than he had. He was in extreme old age when he was assassinated by members of his wife's family.

SIGMUND A hero of the Vikings. *See* Chapter 5.

SIGNY Twin sister of Sigmund (*q.v.*) and wife of Siggeir. She was keen that her sons should grow up to become great warriors, and so she sent her first-born to Sigmund to be tested for courage. The boy failed the test; Sigmund, one of life's sterner dominies, killed him. Signy's second son likewise failed the test but was let off with a caution. She had never been particularly fond of Siggeir, who had committed the

ABOVE *Tenth-century Viking axe, inlaid with silver, from Mammen, Denmark.*

heinous crime of killing her father, Volsung (*q.v.*), as well as nine of her ten brothers, and so now she concluded that her sons by him were all going to be as foppish as the first two. What she needed was a son with the pure blood of Volsung flowing in his veins. She therefore took the form of a beautiful young witch and had three nights of lusty incest with Sigmund. The result was Sinfiotli (*q.v.*).

SIGURD (Siegfried) A hero of the Vikings. *See* Chapter 5.

SIGURD RING King of Ringric who wanted to marry Ingeborg (*q.v.*); he achieved his goal and also extracted a yearly tribute from Helge and Halfdan (*q.q.v.*).

SINFIOTLI The eldest son of Sigmund (*q.v.*); his mother was Sigmund's sister Signy (*q.v.*). Sinfiotli was from the start a brave child, unlike his two elder halfbrothers whom Signy had borne to her husband, Siggeir (*q.v.*): his mother tested his courage by sewing his clothes directly onto his skin and then ripping them away, to which the young hero responded with a merry laugh. Sinfiotli and Sigmund had many adventures together. In one of these they transformed themselves into wolves and savaged everything in sight. They found this such fun that they started savaging each other, and Sinfiotli was killed. Luckily a passing raven gave Sigmund a magic leaf with which he was able to restore his son to life. Sinfiotli later killed the two youngest children of Siggeir and Signy, at Signy's behest. For this murder both he and Sigmund were justifiably sentenced by Siggeir to be buried alive, but Signy delivered Sigmund's magic sword to Sinfiotli and he was able to hack out an exit from their tomb. The pair went to Siggeir's hall and burnt alive all of the men there; the women they allowed to flee – with the exception of Signy, who had decided she didn't want to go on living: just before her death she broke it to Sigmund that Sinfiotli was in fact his son. Sigmund then married Borghild (*q.v.*) who killed Sinfiotli by poison.

SKIDBLADNIR A magical ship commissioned by Loki from the dwarf Dvalin (*q.v.*) as a present to placate Thor and Sif.

SKINFAXI The horse pulling the chariot of Dag (*q.v.*).

SKIOLD A king of Denmark who was in theory one of the sons of the god Odin (*q.v.*); he married Gefjon (*q.v.*).

SKIRNIR A servant of the god Frey (*q.v.*); thanks to the efforts of Skirnir, Frey was able to marry the giantess Gerda (*q.v.*).

SKÖLL The wolf that pursued the Sun. Just before Ragnarok this wolf will succeed in catching the Sun and eating it.

SLAGFINN A brother of Völund (*q.v.*); he raped a Valkyrie.

SLEIPNIR The eight-legged horse belonging to Odin (*q.v.*). In contradiction to common sense, this horse ran very swiftly; you would have expected it to fall over its own extranumery legs. The god Hermod (*q.v.*) was allowed to ride him on occasion; Loki (*q.v.*) was probably its father or even mother – *see* Chapter 3.

SNOR The wife of Karl (*q.v.*).

ABOVE *Asbyrgi, a rock in Iceland supposed to have been a hoofmark made by Sleipnir.*

RIGHT *Eighth-century Swedish stela from Tjängvide, showing Odin's eight-legged steed Sleipnir.*

SOKVABEK (Sokkvabekk) The hall of the goddess Saga (*q.v.*).

SOL The Sun.

SON One of the bowls into which the dwarfs Fialar (*q.v.*) and Galar drained the blood of the god Kvasir, whom they had murdered.

SÖRLI A son of the Valkyrie Gudrun by Jonakur (*q.q.v.*).

SOTÉ A pirate who stole an armlet forged by Völund (*q.v.*).

SVADILFARE (Svadilfari) A horse that helped to put walls around Asgard and, thanks to Loki, sired Sleipnir (*q.v.*).

SVALIN A shield that protected the world from the harshest of the Sun's rays.

SVARTALFHEIM The realm in which lived the dark elves.

SVASUD The father of Summer.

TANNGNIOSTR A goat belonging to Thor; the name means 'tooth cracker'.

TANNGRISNR A goat belonging to Thor; the name means 'tooth gnasher'.

TANNHÄUSER A Teutonic hero who was, apparently, ensnared physically by the goddess Holda, or Frigga (*q.v.*); he found this great fun at the time but then went off to ask absolution from the pope. The pope said that worshippers of heathen gods should accept whatever they were given (in other words, eternal hell-fire) and that Tannhäuser would be forgiven only when the pope's holy staff bore fruit – an impossibility, because the staff was made of dead wood. Tannhäuser was a bit depressed by all this, and so decided to return to Holda's embrace. Three days later the pope's staff began to produce green buds, and a message was sent urgently to Tannhäuser saying that, after all, he was forgiven. Unfortunately the message arrived too late, so Tannhäuser was condemned to spend the rest of eternity making passionate love with Holda.

THIALFI The son of a peasant who, along with his sister Roskva (*q.v.*), was conscripted as a slave by Thor. The boy proved to be one of the more significant members of the Norse pantheon.

THING The Thing was (and still is) a Scandinavian public assembly or law court.

THIR (Thyr) The wife of Thrall (*q.v.*).

THORA Daughter of Hakon and wife of Elf (*q.q.v.*).

THORER Son of Viking and brother of Thorsten (*q.q.v.*).

THORSTEN A hero of the Vikings; a son of Viking and brother of Thorer. *See* Chapter 5.

THRALL The son born of an illicit union between the god Heimdall and the mortal Edda (*q.q.v.*). Thrall was not the most attractive of men but he stirred the heart of Thir (who was not the most attractive of women); they succeeded in giving birth to the race of serfs or thralls.

THRIDI One of the three creatures that spoke with Gylfi (*q.v.*).

THRUDHEIM (Thrudvang) The realm of Asgard in which Thor lived.

TYRFING A magical sword created by the dwarfs and owned by Angantyr (*q.v.*).

UNDINES Friendly female water spirits; they were the Norse equivalents of mermaids.

URD (Urdr) The fountain of the three Norns (*q.v.*).

UTGARD A place in Jotunheim ruled over by Utgard-Loki (*q.v.*).

VALASKIALF (Valaskjalf) Odin's hall in Asgard.

VALHALLA The hall to which warriors went after being slain.

VALI Not to be confused with the god Vali (*q.v.*), this was the son of Loki and Sigyn (*q.q.v.*). He killed his brother Narve (*q.v.*).

VANAHEIM The realm in which lived the Vanir.

VEDFOLNIR The falcon that sat between the eyes of the eagle atop Yggdrasil (*q.v.*) and saw everything that happened in the nine worlds, reporting each event to the gods.

VIGRID The plain in Asgard on which Ragnarok (*q.v.*) will take place.

VIKING A hero of the Vikings. *See* Chapter 5.

VINDSAL The father of Winter and the son of Vasud (*q.q.v.*).

VINGNIR Husband of Hlora (*q.v.*).

VINGOLF A hall in Asgard; here the goddesses met and conversed.

VOLSUNG The father of Sigmund and Signy (*q.q.v.*). He became the king of the Huns after the death of his father Rerir (*q.v.*); he had ten sons and one daughter, Signy (*q.v.*), whose twin brother was Sigmund. *See* Chapter 5.

VÖLUND (Wayland, Weland) The smith captured and hamstrung by Nidud (*q.v.*). *See* Chapter 5.

VON A river that flowed from the mouth of Fenris (*q.v.*).

WALPURGISNACHT The eve of May 1. According to Teutonic myth, on this night the witches associated with the cult of Frey dance on the Brocken (*q.v.*).

YDALIR Hall in Asgard of the god Ull (*q.v.*).

YGGDRASIL (Yggdrasill) The World Tree, an ash that linked all of the nine worlds. It was created by All-father not long after he had created the human race. It had three enormous roots; one in Asgard, one in Midgard and one in Niflheim. It was a haven for wildlife. On its topmost branch, which overshadowed Odin's own hall in Asgard, there rested an eagle between whose eyes sat a falcon called Vedfolnir; a goat called Heidrun wandered about the tree's branches; four stags – Dain, Duneyr, Durathor and Dvalin – did likewise. The dragon Nidhug (*q.v.*) chewed away at the tree's roots. A squirrel called Ratatosk (*q.v.*) ran up and down the tree telling lies about the things the eagle and the dragon had said about each other.

BELOW The Viking–Christian cross at Gosforth, Cumbria, Britain. The carving at the base of the cross is thought to represent Yggdrasil.

TWO

The Creation

In the beginning there was nothing. No, not quite nothing. There was an endless space and a god called Allfather (often confusingly identified with Odin) who was invisible and who had existed for ever. He had eleven other names, ranging from Spear-shaker to Gelding to Ruler of Weather. The huge abyss of emptiness was called Ginnungagap. Long before the Earth was created, there came to exist Yggdrasil, the World Tree, an ash that would link all of the nine worlds.

LEFT *Nineteenth-century book illustration showing Surt, the giant with the flaming sword who guarded the realm of Muspell.*

Under one of its roots, to the south, there was a realm called Muspell, which was so hot that anyone who did not live there would be consumed by the heat; it was guarded by a giant called Surt who was armed with a burning sword. This was a place of fire: embers from it floated down into Ginnungagap. Under another root, to the north, there was a realm called Niflheim, a land of mist and darkness; directly beneath this great root was Hvergelmir, a bubbling cauldron that supplied the waters for twelve huge rivers. In the cauldron there was also a repellent dragon called Nidhug that gnawed away at the roots of the great tree; when it and its wormlike allies succeed in killing the tree, the world will come to an end. The waters of the rivers pouring from Hvergelmir flowed torrentially into Ginnungagap and, as they fell into the frigid void, became great blocks of ice.

Far down, at the base of Ginnungagap, the embers from Muspell dropped onto these piles of ice so that great clouds of steam arose. The steam turned into rime, which progressively filled up Ginnungagap. To the north, near Niflheim, there were gales and a neverending drizzle of cold rain; to the south, near Muspell, the glowing embers lit up the sky as they met the ascending rime. The result was that the centre of the rising surface became a temperate ocean, This was incarnated in the form of an evil giant called Ymir – the first of the ice giants.

The thawing of the rime created also a cow, Audhumla. Her udder gave out four streams of milk, and from these Ymir was able to gain sustenance. The cow licked blocks of salty ice so that, on the first day, the hair of a being appeared; her licking on the second day revealed the head of the being; her licking on the third exposed the entire body of this being, Buri. In the meantime Ymir had been sleeping, and as he slept he sweated; from the sweat of his left armpit were born the first man and the first woman (but see below). Ymir's legs copulated with each other to produce a six-headed giant called Thrudgelmir, who in due course gave birth to Bergelmir, the direct ancestor of the frost giants.

Buri became the forefather of the gods. He had a son, Börr, and the two of them immediately began to battle against the evil giants. The battle lasted for a longer time than human beings can reckon, but then Börr married a giantess called Bestla and sired three great sons – Odin, Vili and Ve.

BELOW A ninth or tenth-century golden arm-ring from Råbylille, Denmark, whose decoration consists of symbols of Yggdrasil.

These three leapt into battle alongside their father, so that soon Ymir was slain. All the giants were drowned in the flood of Ymir's blood except Bergelmir and his mate; these two fled in a longship to a place called Jotunheim, where they bred. The frost giants who descended from Bergelmir and his wife perhaps understandably regarded the gods ever after as their natural foes – even though, on occasion, members of the two factions could exhibit amity.

Odin, Vili and Ve were left with Ymir's corpse, presumably wondering what to do with it. They tugged it out across Ginnungagap and started to chop it up to make the various parts of the physical world. Our world of mortals, Midgard, they manufactured from Ymir's flesh; the giant's blood they used for the oceans and his unbroken bones for the mountains. His broken bones, his teeth and bits of his jaws became the cliffs, rocks and stones of the world. His skull they made into the dome of the sky; to keep it aloft they created four dwarfs (Austri, Nordri, Sudri and Westri), corresponding to the four cardinal points, who supported it. His brains became the clouds. They used the embers from Muspell to create the light that illuminates both heaven and the Earth; they also made the stars and the planets. The three gods then created the first human beings (but see above) out of a pair of trees they discovered: Odin's contributions to these people were life and spirit, Vili's mobility and intelligence, and Ve's the senses.

The first man was called Ask (meaning ash tree) and the first woman Embla (meaning, possibly, elm). Right in the middle of what had now become the world the gods built Asgard: the gods are still living there, and will do so until Ragnarok.

The brightest of the embers from Muspell were given special names and special prominence: they were the Moon (Mani) and the Sun (Sol). These two beings were set by the three gods into chariots that were designed to cross the sky. (An alternative version is that the Moon and Sun were the son and daughter, respectively, of a man called Mundilfari; Sun's husband was a man named Glen or Glaur. The gods were outraged by Mundilfari's impertinence in calling his children by the names of the heavenly lights they had created, and so snatched away the gleaming children to drive the chariots of the Moon and the Sun. It is these children that we see as bright lights in the sky.) The two horses drawing Sol's chariot, Arvakr and Alsvin, had to be protected from Sol's great heat: they were endowed with cooling devices plus the shielding of another device called Svalin. The horse that drew Mani's chariot was called Alsvider. Mani had two attendants, children he snatched up from the ground while they were collecting water from a well. They were called Hiuki and Bil, and represented the waxing and waning Moon.

A giant called Norvi had had a daughter called Nott, or Night. She, in turn, had children by three husbands: Aud was her son by her first husband, Naglfari; Fjorgyn (Jörd; Earth) was her daughter by her second husband, Annar; Dag (Day), an astoundingly beautiful and radiant youth, was her son by her third husband, Dellinger, the god of dawn, a relation of Odin, Vili and Ve. These three gods gave Nott a chariot in which she could circle the heavens; it was drawn by a horse called Hrimfaxi. Later, when they saw the beauty of Dag, they gave him a chariot as well; its horse was Skinfaxi. The mane of Skinfaxi gives off a brilliant light which serves to illuminate the world.

Mani precedes Sol across the sky, but Sol is always in a hurry to catch up. This is because Sol is being pursued by a wolf called Sköll. Mani is likewise being chased by a wolf, Hati. From time to time the wolves succeed in catching their prey, so that the light of the Sun or the Moon is blotted out; however, people on Earth can make enough noise to scare the wolves away and restore the light. In the end, though – just before Ragnarok – the wolves will finally triumph.

The gods appointed various other guardians. The responsibility for the changing of the seasons was divided between Winter and Summer. Winter was the grandson of the god Vasud – the frigid wind – and the son of Vindsval, neither of whom were the sort of progenitor you'd particularly want to meet up a dark alley. Winter took on their nastier characteristics and therefore unreasoningly loathed Summer, who was a son of a benign and lovely god called Svasud. Less important guardians of the regularity of passing time were Noon, Afternoon, Evening, Midnight, Morning and Forenoon.

The three original gods had something of a problem. While they'd been reducing Ymir's body to its constituent parts they'd noticed that the flesh of the giant's body had been crawling with maggots. The gods decided to be merciful to these creatures. They gave them a subhuman form, the nature of which depended upon their spiritual characteristics. Those whose ethics were questionable became dwarfs: they were condemned to live underground, knowing that if they came out into the open during the day they would be instantly turned to stone. (Dwarfs could also be called dark elves, gnomes, kobolds or trolls; whatever the name, they were banished to Svartalfaheim.) The maggots that were considered ideologically sound became fairies and light elves. They had a much better time of it, being given the lovely realm of Alfheim, which was halfway between Heaven and Earth; from here they could flit down to Earth whenever they wanted. Neither of these two classes of being could be considered as human: normally they were deadly enemies, but on occasion they could be friendly towards mortals or gods.

The gods then created their own realm, Asgard, and the realm of mortals, Midgard. All of the worlds were still connected by the trunk of the great ash tree Yggdrasil, whose roots lay in Asgard, Jotunheim and Niflheim. Its topmost bough, Lerad, had perched on it an eagle between whose eyes sat a hawk called Vedfolnir; it was the duty of Vedfolnir to look down over all of Heaven, Earth and Niflheim and report what was happening there. Yggdrasil had other infesting fauna. Aside from Nidhug, chewing at the tree's roots, there were the four deer – Dain, Duneyr, Durathor and Dvalin – that roamed among its branches: the dew dripping from their antlers came together to form the world's rivers. Then there was a squirrel called Ratatosk: it spent its time running up and down the great tree's trunk exchanging malicious gossip between the eagle and the dragon, hoping to make them declare war on each other. The Norns had the daily task of sprinkling water from a blessed well called Urdar down over the branches of Yggdrasil, so that the great tree was constantly refreshed; the water falling from the lower branches became bees' honey.

The family of gods sired by Odin and his brothers was called the Aesir. But there was also another family of older gods, the Vanir, fertility gods whose powers were generally related to those of the wind and the sea; they lived in Vanaheim. Very early on there was a war between the Aesir and the Vanir. The result was a stalemate, and so hostages were exchanged. The Vanir sent Njord to Asgard with his two children, Frey and Freya, and the Aesir sent Mimir and Hoenir, a brother of Odin, to Vanaheim. This disposition of gods seems to have suited everybody, because Frey and Freya became important members of the Norse pantheon, while Hoenir will be one of the very few lucky enough to survive Ragnarok.

Asgard

Asgard was the home of the gods. It was built by Odin and the other gods and goddesses in the very early days. Mortals were unable to see this realm because the plain on which it was sited, Idawold (or Idavoll), floated far above the Earth. A river called Ifing separated Idawald from the rest of the world: its waters were distinguished by the fact that they never froze.

However, there was a link between our mortal Earth and Asgard – the magical bridge called Bifrost, which be equated with the rainbow: its colours were born of fire, water and the air. The gods were able to use this bridge to travel up from and down to Midgard, the world of human beings. One difficulty the gods faced was that their weight might shatter Bifrost: the god Thor therefore eschewed the bridge altogether, while the others trod warily. At the Midgard end of the bridge stood the god Heimdall clutching a horn: every time the gods entered or left Asgard, Heimdall would sound a quiet note on this instrument. When Ragnarok happens he'll sound a loud and savage blast to signify the end of the world.

Asgard was furnished with several halls belonging to the major gods and goddesses. Freya's hall, for example, was called Folkvang; Forseti's was Glitnir; Gladsheim was one of Odin's halls, and was equipped with twelve thrones where the major gods sat in council. Another feature of Asgard was Hlidskialf, the great throne of Odin. From here the great god – or Frigga, because she was allowed to sit on Hlidskialf as well – could see everything that was happening in all of the worlds.

THREE

Tales of Gods
and Goddesses

LEFT *Nineteenth-
century book
illustration depicting
Aegir, god of the sea,
and his wife Ran, who
used her net to snatch
sailors from the decks
of their ships.*

AEGIR AND NJORD

Both Aegir and Njord were gods of the sea; the former was one of the Aesir (if not a member of an even earlier family of gods) and the latter one of the Vanir. In the early days the Norse worshipped Aegir and nodded their heads towards Njord; later they worshipped Njord and barely remembered Aegir as a separate god. During this time the stories of Aegir and Njord became inextricably mixed up with each other. Since the sea was so important to the Vikings, the whole process represented a fairly significant turnaround.

Aegir lived in a hall beneath the sea near the island of Hlesey. He shared the hall with his wife-sister, Ran. Much hated, Ran was the goddess of death for all who perished at sea. Her task was to use a net to haul men from the decks of ships to a watery grave in the hall she shared with her husband-brother. One legend has it that mariners might reappear at their own funeral feasts if Ran had welcomed them to the seafloor with especial enthusiasm. And, even for those less fortunate, her welcome was not neces-

sarily unfriendly: in her seafloor hall the mead flowed as freely as it did at Valhalla, and couches were set out to receive the bodies of the drowned. Sailors who went overboard bearing gold were particularly well received; Ran loved gold, and used its gleam to illuminate the submarine hall. Ran and Aegir had nine beautiful giantess daughters, the Wave Maidens, with whom Odin mated to produce (from all the mothers simultaneously) the god Heimdall.

Aegir himself was one of the brothers of Loki and Kari. He, too, seems to have been unpopular among the Vikings, because of his perceived delight in swooping over the tops of the waves to capsize ships and seize their crews.

Once Aegir and Ran were relaxing in their hall when Thor and Tyr burst in. The gods of Asgard had run out of mead: Thor demanded that Aegir and Ran should swiftly do some brewing to end this shortage. Aegir was not best pleased by Thor's demand, but said that he would try his hardest if Thor could only produce a cauldron or kettle large enough for Aegir to brew sufficient of the stuff. The god replied that this would be no problem, and Tyr chipped in to mention that his father, the giant Hymir, possessed a suitably huge cauldron. Thor and Tyr went to the home of Hymir but found that he wasn't there; instead there were two women. One of these was Tyr's grandmother, now transmuted into a hag with 900 heads. The other was Tyr's mother, and was lovely; she brought the two gods mugs of ale and suggested that, after they'd drunk it, they should conceal themselves under a pair of Hymir's cauldrons; she warned them that his glance was so powerful that it could kill. Almost immediately afterwards, Hymir entered his hall, looking around with a venomous gaze; all of the rafters split except, fortunately, the one that had been supporting the cauldrons hanging over the two gods. Hymir welcomed his visitors and gave them food, killing three cows, two of which Thor ate. The giant was

somewhat upset by this, and told Thor that the following morning they would go fishing together, using their own bait. Thor responded by chopping of the head of one of Hymir's cattle, Himinibrioter, to use as a bait.

The god and the giant rowed out to sea. Thor was looking for the Midgard Snake (Jormungand), and frequently he dipped his fingers beneath the boat to search for it. Even though he had the bull's head, the god was unsuccessful; Hymir, on the other hand, fetched up two whales. Then Thor caught the Midgard Snake, stretching his feet against the base of the ship. His feet went right through, and the giant panicked: he cut the line so that the snake sank back to the depths of the ocean.

Thor, infuriated, hit Hymir with his hammer. The giant was fortunately unharmed and the two of them waded ashore: Thor carried the boat they had been sailing in while the giant carried his two whales. They shared the whales for breakfast. Then the god attempted to prove his strength by throwing a pewter beaker against the giant's forehead. Hymir, impressed by this demonstration, told Thor that he could take away the cauldron. This was how Aegir gained a cauldron large enough to brew mead for all the gods.

Another tale of Aegir concerns the banquet he offered to the gods, whom he invited down to his hall at the bottom of the sea. The gods accepted the invitation happily, but regretted the absence from the feast of Balder. Loki, who had used Hodur to murder Balder, was likewise absent but then, to the gods' dismay, appeared. He took pleasure in slandering them all, Sif in particular.

Njord started off as one of the Vanir; he was brought, along with his children Frey and Freya, to Asgard as a hostage at the end of the war between the Aesir and the Vanir. Like Aegir he was a sea god; his special responsibilities were the sea near to the shore and the wind off the sea, as well as fishing and trade. From his hall, Nôatûn, he worked to calm the tempests created far out at sea by Aegir. Despite the fact that their responsibilities differed, Njord in due course took over the Vikings' allegiance from Aegir – aside from anything else, he was seen as a much more beneficent god than Aegir, even though later he was regarded as responsible for storms at sea, as Aegir had been. He was also thought of as being very handsome, a quality that was never widely attributed to Aegir.

The first wife of Njord was Nerthus; some myths equate Nerthus with Frigga, but this cannot have been true because Nerthus was one of the Vanir. Once Njord came to Asgard he had to look around for a new wife. His prayers were answered when, one day, a young giantess called Skadi arrived in Asgard from her home in Thrymheim. Her father had been the giant Thiassi (see Chapter 1), who had been responsible for kidnapping the goddess Idun; the gods had slain Thiassi after Loki had succeeded in rescuing Idun, and now Skadi wanted some form of reparation. She can be regarded as the Norse equivalent of the Greek Diana: she was associated with hunting and winter. She was also very lovely – but vengeful for the death of her father. The Aesir admitted that she had a valid cause, and offered to give her gold, but she was so furious that she demanded a life in return for the life of her father. The Aesir would have been in trouble had it not been for Loki, who capered and danced (at one point tying his scrotum to a goat) until the giantess's features melted into a smile; the gods then took advantage of her mellowness, pointing to the constellation which they had created from her father's eyes. They added that, rather than kill one of them, she could instead select from among their number a husband – provided that she

would be willing to do so through examination of their naked feet alone. (The chronology of these events in Asgard is given in a different order in different sources.) Perhaps there had been a lot of mead flowing, but she agreed to this condition and looked around for the prettiest pair of feet she could see. And there was a pair of sumptuously formed feet! She assumed they must belong to Balder, the fairest of all the gods, whom she had earlier seen and taken a fancy to. To her horror she discovered that in fact she had selected Njord, and so they had to be married.

In fact, she and Njord had a fine honeymoon in Asgard; all of the Aesir went out of their way to make her feel honoured. Afterwards Njord took her back to Nôatûn – where the trouble started. Although the couple were still fond of each other, Skadi couldn't tolerate the sound of the breakers, the screams of the gulls and the harsh cries of the seals. She told Njord that she would never have another good night's sleep again unless he took her back to Thrymheim. He was so entranced by her that he readily agreed that they could spend nine nights out of every dozen (or nine months of each year – sources differ) there, returning to Nôatûn only for the other three. Unfortunately, he soon came to detest Thrymheim because he was kept awake each night by the din of the frequent avalanches, the whistle of the wind through the pine trees, the crashing of waterfalls, the crackling of the ice and the howling of the wolves.

Njord and Skadi – equated with the summer and the winter – put up with their privations for some time, she spending the three months of summer by the sea and he remaining with her for the other nine months in her home in the mountains. Eventually, though, they agreed that neither of them could put up with the situation much longer, and so they amicably agreed to separate. Long after, Skadi gave birth to Saeming, the first king of Norway; the father was supposed to have been Odin.

BALDER

Balder was the most beautiful of all the gods. He was a son of Odin and Frigga. His twin brother was Hoder but, while Balder, the god of light, was radiantly handsome, poor Hoder, the god of darkness, was blind and gloomy. Nevertheless, the two brothers were deeply devoted to each other, living together in Balder's hall, Breidablik, along with Balder's wife Nanna.

Balder had runes carved on his tongue – indeed, he could read all runes. He was also a master of herbal medicine, and he could see the future – except, that is, for the truth about his own fate. As he walked Asgard, loved by mortals and gods alike, he talked of his dreams, which were always of the best. But then his demeanour began to change: he walked slumpedly and defeatedly, and the light vanished from his eyes. When the gods asked why this was he explained that his dreams had now become nightmares bearing with them a presentiment of some terrible fate awaiting him. Balder's mother and father took his fears seriously, and Frigga determined to do something to ensure her son's safety. She accordingly elicited from every object in the world – animals, plants, stones, ores, everything – a promise that they would not harm Balder. The only thing whose promise was not given was the mistletoe but, as the goddess's minions pointed out, this plant was too soft, young and puny to do the great Balder any serious harm.

The gods then, on several occasions, had fun in Gladsheim by testing Balder's new-found invulnerability. They threw rocks at him, fired arrows at him, struck at him with axes and swords – nothing had any effect, and there was much hilarity. One god, though, was not so pleased. This was Loki, who for long had been jealous of Balder's popularity. He schemed the radiant god's downfall. Knowing that

Frigga had given Balder his apparently complete invulnerability, he nevertheless suspected that there might be a loophole. He therefore changed himself into the form of an old woman and came to Frigga where she sat spinning in her hall. It didn't take him long to discover from the goddess that the mistletoe had failed to be enlisted to her cause.

Loki swiftly left her and went to find a bunch of mistletoe. He stripped away most of the berries and branches to leave one that was long and straight; this he sharpened at one end. He then went to the place where the gods were enjoying themselves throwing objects harmlessly at Balder. Loki's eyes fastened on Hoder, who was doing his

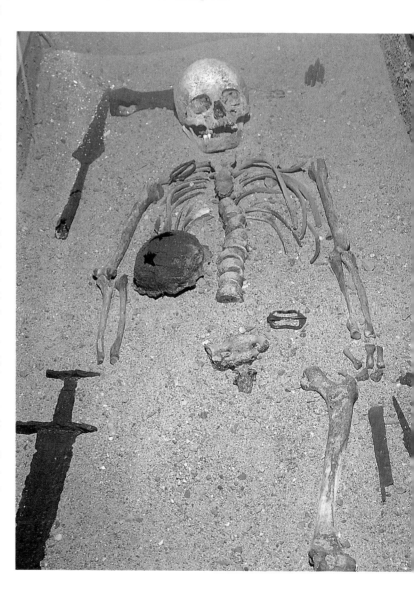

BELOW *To be granted a funeral pyre was a great honour among the Vikings: a lesser honour for a warrior was to be buried alongside his weaponry. Here we see a reconstruction of a grave believed to date from about the tenth century.*

best to join in the fun – but with little success, because of his blindness. He went up to Hoder and offered to help him by guiding his hand if he wanted to throw an object – like this sharpened stick that Loki just happened to have with him. Like a fool Hoder agreed to this plan, threw the dart of mistletoe and killed his brother.

Earlier, Odin, worried like Frigga about Balder's future, had travelled to Hel to consult a prophetess. The prophetess had been interred in the grim otherland for many long years, and was unwilling to stir herself. However, Odin – pretending to be a mortal called Vegtam – used runes and magic spells to force her to answer his questions. He pointed around them to where the denizens of Hel were preparing a feast, and asked who the feast was to be in honour of; she responded that it was being readied to welcome Balder, who would soon be slain by his brother Hoder. Odin was grief-stricken, but found the time to press the prophetess into telling him who would avenge Balder's death. She told him that this would be the task of Vali, a god who would be born to Odin and the earth-goddess Rind. Odin then asked the prophetess a further question: would anyone refuse to weep at Balder's death? She immediately guessed that the person speaking to her had foreknowledge of the future and must therefore be Odin, so she refused to answer this last question and descended once more to her grave. Greatly saddened, Odin returned to Asgard, where he was reassured to discover that Frigga – or so she thought – had extracted the promise of all things not to harm Balder.

When the dart of mistletoe killed Balder the gods were horrified. They could see all too well who had been guilty of the crime – Loki – but at the same time their cruel code dictated that it was Hoder who should die to avenge his brother's death. Nevertheless, it was taboo to shed blood in Gladsheim, and so there was nothing they could immediately do. Frigga, however, was less concerned with

vengeance than with the possibility that Balder might – just possibly – be restored to life. She asked the assembled company if there were any-one there who might risk great peril and travel to Hel to ask the goddess of death if there was any way that she might be bribed into releasing Balder back to the land of the living. There was an embarrassingly long silence at this, because the journey to Hel was by no means a pleasant one, but, eventually, when Frigga promised that the brave volunteer would be considered by herself and Odin to be the dearest of all the Aesir, Hermod stepped forward to say that he would perform the task. Soon he was on his way, Odin having lent him his eight-footed horse Sleipnir for the journey.

Once Hermod had departed, it was the duty of the gods to create Balder's funeral pyre, for which they used his ship, Ringhorn, and vast quantities of wood cut from a nearby forest. The gods each added to the pyre their most treasured possessions. In Odin's case this was his ring called Draupnir. As he added it to the pyre he also whispered some words into the dead Balder's ear, but none of the other gods were near enough to hear what those words were.

The preparation of Balder's pyre was too much for the god's wife, Nanna. She collapsed and died, and so was put on Ringhorn beside her husband, to share his fiery fate.

Unfortunately, the gods had loaded Ringhorn so enthusiastically with precious objects that they found themselves incapable of launching the ship. Luckily the mountain giants, who had been watching the whole proceedings, stepped in to offer help. They told the gods that one of their number, a giant-ess called Hyrrokin, was so strong that she would be able to shove the ship from shore unaided. When the giant-ess was summoned, she arrived riding an enormous wolf, the pacification of which took the company some while. The Hyrrokin put her shoulder to Ringhorn and with a single heave managed to launch it: the rollers down

RIGHT *Hermod, his initial plea to Hel having failed, bids farewell to Balder and Nanna. At this stage Hermod was optimistic, because he believed that all the world would fulfil Hel's condition for releasing the beautiful god by weeping for him. A nineteenth-century book illustration.*

which it ran caught fire from the friction and all the worlds shook from the force of her effort. The gods staggered and Thor, for one, was so incensed by the perceived insult that he prepared to assault the giantess with his hammer; luckily the other Aesir pointed out that she had been helping them, and his anger diminished. But soon afterwards a dwarf called Lit got in Thor's way and the god responded by kicking him, still alive, to perish in the flames of the pyre.

Meanwhile Hermod was on his way to Hel, in Niflheim. Finally he crossed the bridge over the river Giöll to reach the dreaded realm, and there he was stopped by the hideous guard called Modgud. She told him that his clattering across the bridge had made more noise than a whole army of the dead who had ridden over it the day before: it seemed pretty clear to her that he was alive, and she demanded to know who he was and why he had come here. He answered her honestly, and she told him that Balder and Nanna had already arrived; she gave him directions to the gates of Hel itself. These seemed impassable at first, but Hermod spurred Sleipnir into a colossal leap, which whisked both of them safely into Hel.

When he came to Hel's banquet hall, Eljudnir, Hermod found Balder and Nanna. Balder sadly told him that his quest had been at least partly in vain: he was doomed to remain in this place until Ragnarok. However, there was a chance that Hermod could at least take Nanna back to Asgard. But the goddess refused, saying that she preferred to remain with her husband, come what may. Hermod then spoke with the goddess Hel, telling her that all over the nine worlds people were grieving the death of Balder; in this context, he argued, would it not be just to release the god? She thought about this for a time, and then said that she doubted that the grief was quite as universal as Hermod claimed. However, if everything everywhere, living or dead, could prove its sorrow by weeping for the death of Balder she would be prepared to let him and Nanna go. Mind you, should a single person, animal, plant or object refuse to weep, she would hold onto Balder until the end of time. This particular stricture did not much concern Hermod, who knew – or so he thought – that everything and everyone mourned Balder, and so he was happy as he made his way back to Asgard.

Frigga and the other gods sent messengers to every part of the nine worlds to inform all things of what must be done to save Balder. Soon the weeping was universal – even the vilest things of the worlds were sobbing for the loss of the light-god. There was only one dissident, a giantess called Thok. When the messengers told her what she should do she simply mocked them, saying that she'd never much cared for Balder during his life and saw no reason why Hel should not hold onto him forever. Gloomily the messengers returned to Asgard, where at once the gods realized that the news was not good. Soon they guessed that Thok had in fact been Loki in disguise.

Even though Loki had now twice, in effect, murdered Balder, it still seemed to the gods important that Balder's death be avenged by the death of Hoder. Odin therefore paid suit to Rind, a goddess of the frozen earth. She, however, was less than flattered by his attentions, perhaps feeling that it was rather insulting to her that he should merely wish to use her as breeding stock to produce Vali, the avenger of the prophecy. In the end she consented, however, and the eventual result was a baby boy who grew so rapidly from the moment of his birth that on the very first night of his life Vali came to Asgard and slew Hoder with an arrow.

FREY

Frey was one of the Vanir who came to Asgard as a hostage at the end of the struggle between the Vanir and the Aesir; he was the son of Njord and the twin brother of Freya, whom at one point he also married. He was a fertility god and the god of summer, and the cult associated with him seems to have been pretty unpleasant, involving such practices as human sacrifice. His name is often given as Freyr. He was connected with the image of the boar because of his own magical boar Gullinbursti (made by the dwarfs Sindri and Brock at Loki's request); this creature had shining bristles that lit up the world as it flew through the air. Frey also owned the ship Skidbladnir (fashioned by the dwarf Dvalin, again at Loki's request), which could fly through the air and, although large enough to carry all the gods, their horses and their equipment, could, when not in use, be folded up and put in a pocket. Another useful possession was his sword, which under its own motivation would start slaying his enemies as soon as it was drawn from its sheath. His horse was called Blodughofi. His hall was in Alfheim, the realm of the light elves.

Frey is regarded as one of the three major Norse gods – the other two being, of course, Odin and Thor – yet there are surprisingly few tales about him. The most important concerns his love for a frost giantess, Gerda, the daughter of Gymir and Angrboda. Frey first caught sight of her when he was trespassing on Hlidskialf, Odin's great throne from where everything in the nine worlds was visible. Gerda was a figure of pulsating light (she is often associated with the Aurora Borealis, or Northern Lights), and Frey was instantly stricken with lust for her. For ages afterwards he pined, until Njord, worried for his son's welfare, decided to do something about it. Njord summoned his best servant, Skirnir, and told him to find out what was the matter.

Skirnir quizzed Frey and eventually got the truth out of him. The god realized only too well that the union he wanted to seek with Gerda would be unconscionable to gods and mortals alike, yet still he craved her. So he asked Skirnir to go to Gerda and attempt to woo her; the servant agreed on condition that Frey lend him his sword and his horse. He took with him also eleven of the golden apples of eternal youth as well as Odin's magic ring Draupnir.

Blodughofi bore Skirnir swiftly to Jotunheim, where he found that Gymir's hall was surrounded by curtains of coruscating flame; the servant merely spurred the horse to greater speed, and the two of them shot through the fire. They found that the hall was guarded by huge, horrific hounds, who set up such a howling that Gerda was alerted to their arrival.

BELOW *Twelfth-
century tapestry from
Skog Church,
Hålsingland, Sweden,
showing the battle
between Scandinavian
paganism (on the left)
and the insurgent
Christianity (on the
right). The three figures
on the left are believed
to represent the gods
Odin, Thor and Frey.*

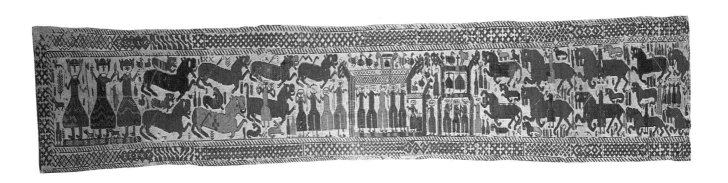

RIGHT *Tenth-century cross fragment found at Michael, Isle of Man, Britain, apparently showing Frey and Gerda. She is probably the birdheaded figure and he the tethered stallion.*

She realized at once that the visitor had been sent by Frey, who had slain her brother Beli in a brawl, but politely asked him in for a horn of mead before sending him on his way. He, however, had other plans, and immediately began to urge Frey's suit – to which she responded forthrightly. Skirnir then tried to bribe her with the apples and with Draupnir, to which she replied in both cases with equal frankness. (The business with the apples, by the way, suggests a link between Gerda and the goddess Idun. It's possible that the two characters were originally one and the same.)

Skirnir abandoned the subtle approach and told her that he would chop her head off if she did not agree to obey Frey's summons. This time she told him that she wasn't scared by his threats and that her father, on getting home, would take great pleasure in taking Skirnir apart. The servant finally used his deadliest threat. Carved on his staff were runes, and he used the magical power of these to lay on her a curse so vile that she was terrified into acquiescence. Refuse and, forever afterwards, he told her, she would be devoured by lust yet remain celibate; be consumed by hunger yet find that all food tasted brackish to her; be confined by Hel's gates and forced to watch that miserable prospect, all the while knowing that she was becoming a repulsive hag. The only way to avoid this miserable fate was to accede to Frey's demands.

This she agreed to do, but said that she would not meet the god for nine nights yet. Frey somehow managed to live through this interminable time and finally the two married. Despite the shocking way in which she had been treated – the whole business, because of the threats, was essentially rape – she came to love him, bearing his child Fiolnir.

A story of the cult of Frey is worth repeating, even though probably quite apocryphal. It was the practice to carry around a carved image of the god on a cart, accompanied by a priestess, so that the faithful could make offerings

and sacrifices to it and therefore ensure good harvests and fertile marriages. It is said that in the 11th century a Norwegian called Gunnar Helming found himself, for some reason, the only person near the cart – apart from the god's lovely young priestess. Helming suddenly had a Good Idea. Thereafter the people visited by the cart were astonished to discover that the wooden figure of the god had miraculously transformed itself into an apparently living young man. The god's enduring characteristic of fertility was in due course evidenced by the changing shape of the priestess. Moreover, this incarnation of the god was willing to walk among mortals and share their food and drink, so they were only too pleased to comply when he suggested that precious gems and coins might make more fitting tributes to him than their previous somewhat tedious offerings and sacrifices. Eventually the Norwegian king, Olaf Tryggvason, heard about this 'miracle', and soon afterwards the god's image became wooden once more.

ABOVE *A bronze
statuette from Lunda,
Sweden, of Frey. His
role as a fertility god is
extremely obvious.*

FREYA

To call Freya a fertility goddess is to euphemize: she was the goddess of sex. Daughter of Njord and twin sister of Frey, she was one of the three Vanir who came to Asgard as hostages at the end of the war between the Vanir and the Aesir; there is some confusion between her and Frigga. The Aesir were so enchanted by her beauty that they granted to her the realm of Folkvang and the hall Sessry-mnir; this latter was so well built that it was regarded as impregnable unless the doors were opened by Freya her-self. Her chariot was pulled either by her boar Hildisvini or by a number of cats. She owned a falcon coat which she could use to fly around the world in the guise of that bird. Horses were involved with her cult, for reasons, it appears, of orgiastic sex. Besides her role in terms of sex and beauty she had a somewhat grimmer aspect, be-cause she often led parties of Valkyries down to fetch the dead from battle-fields, bringing them back to her hall so that they could enjoy all the benefits of the afterlife.

Her first husband was called Od (or Odur), but he deserted her, and there-after she wept golden tears of grief at all opportunities – such as there were, for her life thereafter was one of un-bridled promiscuity. Counting her various conquests is a fraught matter, but we can list her brother Frey (it's possible that the two of them were originally a single god, and that the tale of their sexual relations represents an explanation of the way that, by the time the Eddas were being written, they had become two), Odin and other gods, a man called Ottar (*see* Chapter 1), not to mention four very important dwarfs – see below. When, at his *flyt-ing*, Loki cast certain doubts upon her virtue, it is hard not to agree with his accusations. The gods were not alone in looking on her with a merry grin: the giant Hrungnir, during his bet with Odin, admitted that, while he'd prefer Sif, he'd be quite happy to make do with Freya. She did have her standards, though: she refused to sleep with Hrungnir and likewise with the giant Thrym, even though in the case of the latter she was encouraged to do so by Loki and Thor.

Thrym had stolen Thor's hammer, which was bad news for the gods of Asgard. Loki borrowed Freya's falcon skin and flew over the world to try to ascertain who the thief might be; at last he discovered that the culprit was this rather unprepossessing giant, who said that he had buried Miölnir many miles beneath the surface of the Earth and would not surrender it until Freya had been delivered up to him as his bride. Loki thought this was a fair exchange and so, on his return to Asgard, he proposed it to Freya, sec-onded by Thor. Freya's fury was spec-tacular to behold, so the gods had to try another tack.

Heimdall came up with a possible solution. He pointed out that the problem was really Thor's and Loki's, and that therefore they should have the responsibility for solving it. He suggested that Thor should dress in Freya's clothing and pretend to be her; Loki should likewise dress in female garb and act as 'Freya's' handmaiden. This the two gods rather reluctantly did, and then they journeyed in a goat-drawn chariot back to Thrym's hall.

The giant – presumably myopic – took the gods to be the beautiful women they pretended they were, and welcomed them to a wedding banquet attended by many other giants and giantesses. He was a little disconcerted when 'Freya', at dinner, demolished an ox, eight large salmon, two barrels of mead and all the sweet dishes set out, but Loki explained that this feat had come about simply because 'Freya' had been pining for Thrym for days, and hadn't been able to eat a thing. Next Thrym tried to steal a kiss from 'Freya' but was rocked backwards on his feet by the glare he received from his putative bride. Not to worry, explained Loki: that was just a burning look of passion. The giant's sister asked about the dowry but was ignored: Thrym was convinced that a night of mad ecstasy awaited him. He called for the hammer and commanded that it be placed between 'Freya's' knees as a symbol of their marriage. This was a foolish mistake, because Thor proceeded to use Miölnir to slaughter not only Thrym but also every other giant and giantess on the premises.

Freya's exploits with the four dwarfs involved her more directly. She was exploring the world one night when she came across the smithy of four dwarfs called the Brisings, or Brosings. They were in the process of making an ornament (the Brisingamen, generally assumed to have been a necklace) of such exquisite beauty that Freya could hardly believe her eyes: gems and polished metals mingled and glimmered so that it seemed almost to be liquid flame. There was nothing that the goddess would not do to possess that treasure: when the dwarfs declared that she could have it only if she spent a night of lust with each of them in turn she readily assented.

What she hadn't realized was that Loki had seen her leaving Asgard and had followed her. The wizard of lies rushed to tell Odin of her prostitution, and the king of the Aesir was furious – he longed for Freya himself, so to discover that she was disporting herself with four dwarfs hurt him grievously. At the same time, though, the bulk of his wrath was reserved for Loki, the malicious messenger bearing bad news. He told Loki that he was to steal the Brisingamen from Freya: otherwise there would be terrible punishments in store. Loki pointed out that her hall Sessrymnir could be entered only with Freya's permission, and that the command was therefore an unfair one, but Odin's only response was to become even more threatening, so Loki decided that he would do his best.

The wizard of lies had the advantage that he could change his shape at will. It took him a long time before he discovered a tiny aperture through which he could squirm his way into Sessrymnir, but in the end he managed it. There he saw the lovely form of Freya sprawled on her bed but, alas, in such a position that he was unable to reach the clasp of the Brisingamen. He fidgeted and fumbled for a while and then turned himself into a flea; lighting on Freya's breast he bit her, so that she turned over in her sleep, exposing the clasp. Loki swiftly returned to his own form and let himself out of Sessrymnir, taking the Brisingamen.

What happened next is a matter of debate. According to some versions, the god Heimdall – who could hear even grass growing – heard Loki as he was perpetrating the theft and pursued him. The two waged a battle involving considerable shape-shifting until Loki was finally persuaded that, if he valued his life, he should return the Brisingamen to Freya. An alternative is that Loki, as instructed, took the necklace to Odin, who accepted it. When, next morning, Freya discovered the loss of her treasure, she realized that the only possible culprit had to be Loki, and so she went straight to Odin to complain, saying that if he had had anything to do with the theft he was ... well, the women of the Norse myths could, as ever, be blunt. His response was not unreasonable: she was calling him a degenerate, yet had she not debased herself by whoring to the dwarfs in order to obtain the Brisingamen? He therefore charged her that, by way of punishment, she should in future adopt as part of her responsibilities the spreading of warfare and misery – otherwise he would keep the Brisingamen forever. Freya was ashamed, but agreed to the bargain: she needed the necklace almost more than she needed her life itself.

Freya, as noted, was no paragon of virtue. It might have been expected that she should have been reviled for her sexuality – especially in a primitive society, where women are commonly expected to be both chaste and willing. Yet she was one of the most important and respected members of the Norse pantheon. Possibly the Vikings recognized a sexual equality – a *fairness* in their attitudes towards the behaviour of the two different sexes – that might well be adopted by many of the 'developed' societies of today.

FRIGGA

S econd wife of Odin and mother of Balder, Frigga was the most important goddess in the Norse pantheon. Because of her connection with fertility, there was obviously a marked overlap between her responsibilities and those of Frey and Freya. It seems likely that all three initially had the same identity before Frigga was separated from Frey/Freya and then these two likewise became divided from each other. However, the chronology of all this is hard to establish: in some bran-

ches of Teutonic myth Frigga and Freya are regarded as identical – both, for example, have falcon skins that they can wear to fly around the nine worlds – yet Frey has his own personality. However, Frigga seems always to have been a much gentler fertility goddess than Freya: where the latter represented rampant sex and was associated with a good deal of violence, Frigga was much more associated with that aspect of fertility related to placid domesticity, conjugal happiness and maternity – she was often represented with a bunch of keys at her waist, the symbol of the good housewife. It should not be assumed, however, that she was a consistently obedient spouse: the myths suggest that, early on, she enjoyed adultery with Odin's brothers Vé and Vili and later, often enough, she would work to trick Odin in order to advance the cause of someone she preferred. Frigga's hall was called Fensalir, and she spent much of her time sitting there spinning golden thread or brightly coloured clouds.

Her parentage is something of a conundrum. According to some versions she was the daughter of Odin and the very early goddess Jörd; alternatively she was Jörd's sister, both of them being daughters of the giantess Fiorgyn. Either way, she became Odin's wife and, alone among all the other deities, was permitted to sit upon Hlidskialf, his great throne from which one could see everything that was going on in all the worlds. In addition to this shared omniscience she had also the ability to foretell the future, but she was ever loth to tell what she saw there. She was, perhaps, a little too fond of glorious attire for her own good, but that seems to have been her only notable sin.

It was a sin that could get her into trouble, though, as we discover from one tale (which bears strong resemblances to the story of Freya and the Brisingamen). Odin had had erected a statue of himself and, never modest, had placed a piece of gold inside it. Frigga was keen to have made for her by the dwarfs a magnificent necklace,

LEFT *Nineteenth-
century book
illustration showing
Frigga with some of her
handmaidens. These
handmaidens were
goddesses in their own
right.*

and so she stole the piece of gold for the dwarfs to use. The product of their labours was of amazing beauty – so much so that Odin fell even further in love with her than he had been before. However, he was less than amused when, a little later, he discovered that it had been made from gold stolen from his statue. He immediately summoned the dwarfs and demanded that they tell him who was the thief, but they refused to betray the secret. Odin next composed runes so that the statue would be given the power of speech: it was to be placed high on a gate, and sooner or later would tell the truth of the theft to the world.

Frigga was terrified to hear of all this. She summoned her attendant Fulla and instructed the hapless servant to find some way of avoiding Odin's discovery of the crime and his subsequent wrath. Fulla soon returned in the company of a revoltingly ugly dwarf, who promised that he would stop the statue from speaking if Frigga would sleep with him. Hardly sooner said than done, and the following morning the dwarf went to the gate, magically made the guards fall into a deep sleep and shattered the statue, so that Odin would never be able to reconstitute it and discover the truth it was willing to tell.

RIGHT *A superb animal head, probably from the bow of a Viking longship, discovered during recent dredging of the River Scheldt, Belgium.*

Odin was furious, and he left Asgard and his favourite wife for seven long months. During this time, perhaps assuming that Odin had abdicated his throne, Ve and Vili took power – and also, according to some sources, enjoyed Frigga's sexual favours. However, they did not have the powers of Odin, and so both Asgard and Midgard were mightily relieved when the great god returned to reassume his throne.

Frigga and Odin often walked Midgard together – although she was a much less frequent traveller than he was. A major legend of one of these ventures concerns Agnar and Geirrod (*see* Chapter 1); here Frigga successfully tricked her husband. Another tale of her wiles concerns a war between the Vandals and the Winilers – a war that the heavenly couple had watched with interest from Hlidskialf. Odin was very much on the side of the Vandals, whereas Frigga much preferred the Winilers. One night Frigga asked Odin which of the two sides would win the war on the morrow and he, evasively, said that it would be whichever he first saw. His stratagem was that, because of the direction in which his couch was turned, the first army to meet his gaze would necessarily be that of the Vandals. But he hadn't reckoned with Frigga's cunning. She simply waited until he was fast asleep and then turned his bed around the other way. Sure enough, when Odin awoke he saw the Winilers and, a man of honour, he gave them the victory.

Frigga is identified with many other goddesses in various mythologies. A complete list would be impossible: here we can note Bertha, Brechta, Eástre (from which the term 'Easter' comes), Gode, Hlodin, Holda, Horn, Nerthus (who also features in the Norse pantheon), Ostara and Wode. As the archetypal Earthmother, of course, she has parallels in almost all mythologies.

HEIMDALL

Heimdall is a somewhat enigmatic member of the Norse pantheon, in that it is unclear whether he was a member of the Aesir or of the Vanir. The identity of his father is uncertain (it was probably Odin), but his mothers were nine giantesses called the Wave Maidens (*see* Chapter 1), themselves daughters of Aegir, who together managed to produce this single son. A gynaecological mystery. Heimdall, the White God, the Golden-Toothed, had a trumpet called the Giallar-horn whose tone could be heard throughout the nine worlds; he will use it to announce the onset of Ragnarok. This instrument symbolized the crescent Moon; the god sometimes hung it on one of Yggdrasil's branches and other times put it in Mimir's well, where it lay alongside Odin's lost eye, a symbol of the full Moon. His hall in Asgard was called Himinbiorg and his horse Gull-top (Gold-tuft). He was regarded as the epitome of beauty, brightness, wisdom and goodness.

Heimdall had the task of guarding the rainbow bridge Bifrost to stop the giants attempting to invade Asgard. In order to make this job easier, the gods gave him incredibly acute senses – a sparrow falling would have sounded like a thunderclap to him, because he could hear the wool growing on a sheep's back – and the ability to require little or no sleep. In addition, along with Bragi, he welcomed heroes to Valhalla.

Clearly Heimdall shared many of the attributes of Balder. He also had, like Odin, a habit of wandering among mortals and siring children. In so doing, he started off the lines of the three different classes of human beings. The three legends involved are very much the same. In the first of them, Heimdall – pretending to be a mortal called Riger or Rig – visited a rickety old hut where a husband and wife called Ai (Great Grandfather) and Edda (Great Grandmother) lived. They invited him in for a fairly un-palatable meal, and he ended up stay-ing with them for three nights. Each night he slept between the couple on their bed, and presumably Ai was a sound sleeper because, nine months later, Edda gave birth to Heimdall's son Thrall. The boy was not the most physically prepossessing of fellows, but he was mightily strong and was willing to work from dawn until dusk. He mar-ried a woman called Thir who was like-wise a willing worker and soon they gave birth to a plentiful brood of child-ren, who were the first members of the class of serfs.

Meanwhile Heimdall had been repeating exactly the same act else-where. Afi (Grandfather) and Amma (Grandmother) welcomed him for three nights in similar circumstances, although the food was somewhat better and certainly there was plenty of it. Nine months later a boy called Karl appeared; he proved to be an excellent farmer and, with his wife Snor, who was prudent and, it seems, notable for the ampleness of her bosom. Their children became the first of the peasant class.

The food was much better when Heimdall stayed three nights with Fadir (Father) and Modir (Mother); the accompanying wines were first-class, too. Perhaps for these reasons, the result of the clandestine mating, Jarl, was delicate, handsome and refined.

He soon learned to use the runes and to be very good at killing people; he and his aristocratic wife Erna became the ancestors of the ruling and warrior classes. The youngest of their children was a boy called Konur or Kon, who was if anything even more remarkable than his father. He had the strength of eight men and could speak with the birds, douse fires, still the sea, blunten blades and ease troubled hearts. Un-fortunately, because of the fragmented nature of the surviving manuscripts we know little more about Konur except

BELOW *Part of a carved cross slab found at Jurby, Isle of Man, Britain, depicting Heimdall blowing his horn to summon the gods to Ragnarok.*

that he, or one of his descendants, became the first king of Denmark.

Heimdall's wisdom was useful to the Aesir. When the giant Thrym demanded to have Freya as his bride if he were to return Thor's hammer, it was Heimdall who proposed the plan whereby Thor and Loki travelled in female garb to Thrym's hall. In fact, he seems to have been a champion of Freya's somewhat frail virtue, because there are fragments of another myth in which he wrestled with Loki for the return to her of the Brisingamen. The two gods indulged in a battle of shape-changing (a version of which, fought between Merlin and Madam

BELOW *Detail of an eighth-century stela found in Gotland, Sweden, showing a Scandinavian warrior on horseback.*

Mim, appeared in the 1963 Disney movie *The Sword in the Stone*). Loki became a flame and Heimdall a cloud to rain on him; Loki became a polar bear and prepared to swallow the water but Heimdall became another bear and attacked him; both of them became seals and struggled in the water, with Heimdall being the eventual winner. As he will be in the very last resort: Loki, bound until Ragnarok, will eventually be slain by Heimdall, although the White God will lose his own life at the same time.

IDUN

I dun, the wife of Bragi, was the goddess of Spring and the guardian of the gods' eternal youth. This youthfulness was incorporated in the form of golden apples, which she kept in a magic basket; no matter how many apples she removed from the basket to give to the gods during their feasting there was always still the same number left. Idun reserved her apples exclusively for the gods, who therefore remained young and vigorous while all other beings grew old and died. Naturally the apples were coveted by the dwarfs and giants, and this fact led to Idun's major adventure.

Odin, Hoenir and Loki were one day wandering in the world when they became hungry. Spotting a nearby herd of cattle they promptly killed one of the beasts, made a fire and roasted it. However, when in due course they kicked away the embers of the fire and sat down to eat they discovered that the ox was hardly cooked at all. They tried again, but still without success. At that moment a huge eagle spoke to them, saying that its magic had been stopping the flames from cooking the flesh, and offering the three Aesir a deal: the eagle would remove the spell so that the gods could cook their dinner, but they were to give the bird as much to eat as it wanted. This seemed fair enough to the Aesir, and the bargain was struck.

They hadn't reckoned on the eagle's appetite. It took the shoulder joints and the rump of the ox for its own portion, leaving the gods with not very much. This drove Loki into a fury, and he picked up a branch and plunged it into the bird's back. The eagle dropped the meat and flew off, still impaled by the branch, which Loki now found his hands were stuck to. Low over the ground they flew, so that Loki was bumped and dragged along, being bruised and battered and cut and torn until he was in agony. He screamed for mercy, and finally the bird agreed that it would release him if he would promise to do something for it: lead Idun out from the safety of Asgard so that she could be captured. Loki rapidly agreed to do this and the eagle – who was in fact a giant called Thiassi in disguise – let him go.

Some while later Loki went to Idun and told her that he had discovered a grove where apples grew that were in every respect like her magic ones. Credulously she accepted his offer to lead her to this place. However, as soon as they were out of Asgard he deserted her. Thiassi, again in his guise as an eagle, swooped down from the skies and carried the goddess away to his hall, crowing that at last he had captured the gift of eternal youth. He was deeply chagrined to discover that Idun – although she had always seemed such an ineffectual goddess – refused to let him have a single apple.

It was not long before things at Asgard began to go badly wrong. The Aesir, who had initially assumed the Idun had gone away with her minstrel husband Bragi on one of his ramblings, became very worried about her, especially when they started wrinkling with age and losing their reason to senility. Odin summoned the Aesir to a conference, and when they were gathered they discovered that all were present except Loki. Even their aging brains didn't take long to work out that the wizard of lies had been up to some more of his mischief, and their suspicions were confirmed when one of the servants of Heimdall announced that, the last time he'd seen Idun, she'd been going over Bifrost with Loki.

The other gods made it plain to Loki in no uncertain manner that, unless he got them out of this mess – and quickly – his end was not going to be an enjoyable one. He therefore borrowed Freya's falcon-skin and flew off to Thiassi's hall, Thrymheim. Luckily the giant wasn't there. Loki turned Idun into a nut and, clutching her in his claws, flew back towards Asgard.

When Thiassi returned and found the goddess gone he was furious. At once he adopted the form of a huge eagle once more, and set off in hot pursuit of Loki. And so it was that, when the gods looked out from Asgard to watch for Loki's return, they saw not only the falcon but also, in chase, the great black eagle. The Aesir swiftly gathered up a great heap of fuel. As the falcon flopped exhaustedly into Asgard bearing its precious burden, they set light to the fuel so that Thiassi flew straight into a wall of flames. Burnt and stunned, the eagle crumpled to the ground, where it was swiftly despatched by the Aesir. Later, however, mellowed by a feast of apples and feeling young and fresh again, they threw Thiassi's eyes up into the sky to form a constellation, a tribute which they reckoned would placate any vengeful relatives of the dead giant. (They thought wrong. His daughter Skadi came to Asgard to demand recompense. However, she relented and instead ended up marrying Njord.)

Another legend about Idun has largely been lost to us. It seems that one day she accidentally fell into Niflheim where she went into a frozen and horrified coma. Odin sent Bragi and a couple of the other gods down there after her with some skins to warm her, but they were unable to get her to respond. In the end Bragi told the other two to leave them there, and that he would keep his wife company until she was ready to go. What happened next is, sadly, unrecorded.

LOKI

There are far more tales about Loki than about any of the other gods. The reader is referred to the index for reference to those legends involving Loki that are not discussed here.

Loki, the wizard of lies, the god of mischief and deception, is the most fascinating of all the members of the Norse pantheon, not just because of his wiles and cunning but because he shows that rarest of things in a mythological personage, character development. Although never to be trusted, in the early days he helped Odin create the world and then was useful to the other gods on countless occasions. Later his mischief took on a more malevolent nature, as when he chopped off the hair of Sif (q.v.). But he then became actively evil, arranging for the murder of Balder (q.v.) and committing other hideous crimes – as we shall see.

Loki married three times. His first wife was called Glut and she bore him

67

RIGHT *The western face of Gosforth Cross, Cumbria, Britain, which dates from the tenth century. At the bottom is the chained Loki beneath the serpent; Sigyn, above the serpent, is catching the venom in a cup. Above this scene is Odin, and at the top we see Heimdall being attacked by two dragons.*

the children Einmyria and Eisa; all three names refer to fire and its warmth, since in one of his aspects Loki was the charming god of the fireside, relaxation and leisure. For this reason the peasant classes maintained he was the greatest of all the gods – understandably, because the few moments of leisure they had must have been as precious as gold dust to them. The offspring of his second marriage were less pleasant. This time his wife was a giantess called Angrboda, and their children were Hel, the goddess of death, Jormungand, the World Serpent, and Fenris, the monstrous wolf who came to threaten the very existence of the gods. Loki's third wife was the beautiful Sigyn; their two children were Narvi and Vali (not to be confused with the god called Vali).

As noted, Loki could be very useful to the gods. One such instance occurred when they made a foolish promise. A giant came to Asgard and offered to build a protective wall around it. There was some haggling over his fee, but eventually the gods agreed that he could have the hand of Freya if he could complete the task within a single winter, six months – something they believed to be impossible. Their reasoning was that they could get at least part of the wall built for nothing, saving themselves a deal of hard work. They hadn't reckoned on the giant's horse, a doughty animal that was capable of performing prodigious feats of labour, never ceasing by night or day. As time passed, it began to dawn on the gods that it was very likely that the giant might indeed succeed in his task; then they realized that it was a certainty, and, not wishing to lose Freya, they turned to Loki for help. The last morning of the six months came and there were only a few stones left to be put in place. Then out from Asgard danced a sexy little mare; she whinnied suggestively at the giant's horse and then, with a swish of her tail, danced off into the forest. Suddenly the giant didn't have his equine assistant any longer, and saw that he had no chance of finishing the wall.

He was dejected about having been cheated, and Thor killed him. When the mare returned to Asgard she was the proud mother of a foal, the eight-legged horse Sleipnir, which became Odin's mighty steed.

Another instance of Loki's helpfulness occurred when the giantess Skadi came to Asgard seeking vengeance for the slaying of her father Thiassi. Loki entertained her with lewd knockabout humour until she relented and became the wife of Njord (q.v.).

The trickster could also befriend humans. A peasant gambled on a game of chess with the giant Skrymsli: if the giant won his prize was to be the peasant's son, unless the boy could be hidden so well that he could not be found. And, of course, the giant did win. The grief-stricken peasant turned to Odin for help, and the god changed the lad into a tiny grain of wheat. However, Skrymsli immediately saw through this subterfuge, went to the field in which the boy was concealed and mowed the wheat until at last he came to the right grain. Odin snatched it from his hand at the last moment, returned the boy to his parents and then lost interest in the whole matter. Next the peasants turned to Hoenir, who transformed the boy into a tiny down feather which he placed on the breast of a swan. Again the giant saw through the trick, and would have eaten the down feather had not Hoenir puffed it away from his mouth.

Like Odin, this god then lost interest, so the peasants begged Loki to assist them. He turned the boy into a single egg in a fish's roe. Skrymsli managed to see through this ruse as well, and after some inspired angling was able to draw from the sea the very fish in which the boy was hidden. The giant was picking through the roe looking for the correct egg when Loki snatched it from his grasp and ran away with it. He turned the egg back into the boy again, and told him to flee for home but to make sure, as he did so, to pass through the boathouse where Loki, having taken precautions against failure, had rigged up a sharp spike.

The boy did as he was told and ran off, and Skrymsli, chasing him, seriously injured himself.

Loki chopped off one of the giant's legs but almost immediately it began to join back on to Skrymsli's torso. Swiftly the god realized that there was magic at work, so he chopped off Skrymsli's other leg and this time placed flint and steel between the limb and the body, thus rendering the magic inoperative, so that the giant bled to death.

But Loki could be randomly cruel. One day he, Odin and Hoenir were out walking when Loki spotted an otter by a riverbank preparing to eat a salmon. The god threw a stone accurately and killed the animal, claiming its salmon for the trio's meal. However, this was no ordinary otter: it was Otter, one of the sons of the dwarfish king Hreidmar. So began the whole miserable business of Andvari's gold, mentioned in Chapter 1.

As we saw, Loki's children by the giantess Angrboda were Hel, Jormungand and Fenris. The marriage had been unauthorized and so he tried to

ABOVE *Part of a Viking cross slab at Maughold, Isle of Man, Britain, showing Loki crouching with the stone with which he is about to kill Otter (with salmon in mouth).*

69

RIGHT *Thorwald's Cross Slab, at Andreas, Isle of Man, Britain, dating from about the tenth century and showing Odin being attacked by Fenris at Ragnarok.*

keep the children hidden in a cave, but they grew very rapidly and so it wasn't very long before Odin discovered their existence. The father of the gods determined to get rid of them before they grew so large that they threatened all the world. He cast Hel into Niflheim, in which dismal realm she reigned gloomily as the goddess of death. The snake Jormungand he threw into the sea, where it grew so huge that soon it encircled the entire world and was able to swallow its own tail. Odin was rather alarmed that Loki's offspring could grow so prodigiously, and he looked at Fenris with new nervousness. Might it not be a good idea to try to educate the wolf into the ways of gentleness? He brought Fenris to Asgard.

The gods were terrified of the beast – all except Tyr, the god of courage, who was therefore given the task of tending him. Still Fenris continued to grow in both size and ferocity. The gods were unwilling to kill the wolf, which had been brought to Asgard as a guest, so they decided to bind him so securely that he would never be able to threaten them again. They got hold of a strong chain called Laeding and set to work. Fenris just grinned: he was confident in his own strength, so he waited until they had finished and then casually snapped the chain into a million pieces. The gods tried again with an even stronger chain, Droma, but the result was much the same, although this time Fenris had to struggle a little harder and longer.

A servant of Frey's called Skirnir was sent to ask the dwarfs to make a tether so strong that nothing could ever break it. They gave him a slender strand, Gleipnir, made out of the sound of a cat's footfall, the voice of a fish and other such intangibles. The gods told Fenris that surely, after his exploits with the chains, he couldn't be scared of embarking on this new test of his strength, but he had inherited some of his father's wiliness and looked at it suspiciously, eventually agreeing to be tied up in it only if one of the gods would put a hand in

his (Fenris's) mouth as an earnest that no magic was involved. Nobody was willing to do this except Tyr, who lost his hand when the secured Fenris discovered that he had been duped.

The wolf was then placed beneath the ground, but he howled with such abandon that the gods couldn't stand the noise. To silence him the Aesir put a sword vertically in his mouth, with its point in his palate; blood flowed forth to form a great river. And so Fenris will stay until Ragnarok, when Gleipnir will be sundered and he can exact his revenge on the gods. There is an interesting parallel here with Loki's own fate, as we shall see.

Loki's tricks became more and more spiteful. With his lies and his habit of revealing secrets he constantly stirred the gods against each other. One of his worst tricks was the shearing of Sif's (q.v.) magnificent hair. It was as a result of this and his wager with Brock and Sindri that Loki suffered the agonies of having his lips stitched up. The gods' lack of sympathy for – indeed, their merriment over – his torment was probably what turned his petty maliciousness into a vindictive lust to destroy them.

Balder (q.v.), of course, he did destroy, and thereafter he decided that it would be prudent not to show his face in Asgard for a while. The gods were grief-stricken. In order to try to cheer them up a bit, the sea-god Aegir threw a banquet; naturally enough, Loki was not on the guest list. However, he turned up anyway, contributing to the merriment by murdering one of Aegir's servants and insulting all of the gods in the most vitriolic terms, as recorded in a riveting *flyting* ('insult poem'). Their wrath was intensified by the fact that many of the insults were all too true. Freya, for example, he labelled as a whore because she had slept with the entire male pantheon (including her own brother), uncountable dwarfs, and so on; her response was to tell him that he was lying – but for once, of course, he wasn't. The diatribe continued until Thor threatened to hammer him to death, at which he fled.

The gods decided that enough was enough: something had to be done about Loki. They decided to bind him, much as they had his son Fenris. But first, of course, there was the task of finding him.

Loki was all too well aware that the Aesir would try to track him down. Although he lived quietly in a little shack, he knew that Odin's all-seeing eyes would be able to spot him. He therefore determined that, should the gods come to seek him out, he'd jump into a nearby river and take the form of a salmon. Then he began to worry that the other Aesir might catch on to this ruse: a hook he could, as a highly intelligent salmon, avoid with ease – but what if they used a net? Most nets he would have little trouble in breaking, but perhaps they could make one especially strong … The thought nagged away at him. He reckoned that he was the cleverest of the gods: if *he* couldn't make such a net then none of the others would be able to. In an attempt to set his mind at rest he gathered cord and set to work.

To his alarm he found that it would indeed be possible to make a net capable of catching him. He was halfway through the task when he perceived that Odin, Thor and Kvasir were approaching his shack. In a panic, he threw the half-finished net on the fire to destroy the evidence, ran off and jumped into the river.

The three vengeful gods looked around the empty shack. It seemed that Loki had left no trace of where he had gone to, but then Kvasir, the wisest of all the gods (*see* Chapter 1), spotted the stranded ashes of the burnt net. After a little thought, he realized that Loki must have turned himself into a fish, and suggested that the trio quickly weave a net and trawl the river.

The first time they threw the net Loki was able to escape: he put himself between two stones so that the net couldn't reach him. The three gods had an inkling that this might have been his stratagem, and so, next time around, they weighted the net. Loki avoided it by jumping over it against

RIGHT *The southern face of Gosforth Cross, Cumbria, Britain. Here we can see, at the bottom, the bound Fenris; above is Odin on horseback.*

BELOW *Made from walrus ivory around 1135–1150 and found on the Isle of Lewis, Scotland, these pieces come from a Viking chess set.*

the current, something fish had heretofore never been able to do. However, his leap was seen by the gods, and so they tried again with the weighted net. This time, as Loki jumped over it, Thor was ready and waiting and was able to catch him by the tail.

The three of them dragged him away to bind him – both as punishment for his crimes and to ensure that never again would he plague them. They took him to a deep cavern. Believing that the sins of the fathers should be visited on the children, they induced Loki's son Vali to become a wolf and rip out the throat of his other son, Narvi. From Narvi's corpse they extracted the entrails, and these they used to tie up Loki to three great rocks; as an afterthought they turned the guts into iron, to make doubly sure that Loki would be unable to escape until Ragnarok. Skadi – the giantess whom

Loki had charmed so long ago – decided that his fate hadn't been nearly nasty enough. She fetched a serpent and hung it over Loki's head, so that its venom would drip, second after second, into his face for the rest of eternity – until Ragnarok. Naturally, every drop of venom caused him unspeakable pain. Sigyn, Loki's wife, was not only beautiful but also virtuous and faithful. She could have gone back to Asgard, and enjoyed the life of the gods, but instead she resigned herself to staying beside her husband for all the rest of time, catching the drips in a cup held above his face. She is still there. From time to time, however, the cup becomes filled and she has to empty it. During those moments the venom falls onto Loki's face and he screams in agony.

Come Ragnarok, the gods will regret their cruelty.

RIGHT *Nineteenth-century book illustration of Odin's wild hunt; traditionally Odin rode on eight-legged Sleipnir for this, but here we can see that the artist has omitted the extra four legs. Gales were considered to be the physical manifestations of Odin leading his wild hunt across the sky.*

ODIN

Odin is often called Allfather, which is the name of the primordial deity who initiated the Creation; in fact, in many of the legends it is assumed that the two gods are one and the same. (The roles played by both Allfather and Odin or by Allfather/Odin in the Creation are discussed in Chapter 2.) This may seem like an inconsistency in the mythology – and probably is – but we should remind ourselves that there is a parallel in Christianity, where Christ is both God and the son of God. A further resemblance to this situation is found in a legend relating how Odin, pierced by a spear, was hanged for nine days and nights from a branch of Yggdrasil as a sacrifice to himself. During this time he learned great wisdoms and invented the runes; he became the patron god of hanged men.

There are many tales in this book about Odin: the reader is referred to the index for most of them. Here we shall look at only a few.

Odin required no food, although he would partake of the gods' heavenly mead. His spear was Gungnir, which always found its mark; in addition, it had the property that any oath sworn upon it could never be broken. He owned the magical golden ring called Draupnir: every ninth night this would shed eight replicas of itself. His steed Sleipnir, a son of Loki (q.v.), had eight legs and could travel at colossal speed all over the nine worlds. His high throne in Asgard was called Hlidskialf, and when seated on it Odin could see everything that happened anywhere; Frigga (q.v.), his second wife, was allowed to sit here also. (His other two wives were Jörd and Rind.) Further information from the worlds was brought to him by his two ravens, Hugin and Munin, who flew from Asgard each morning and returned each evening. He was the master of

LEFT *Nineteenth-century book illustration depicting Odin and a group of beautiful valkyries welcoming a dead hero to Valhalla. Notice the two ravens and the two wolves.*

LEFT *From the ninth
century, the skull of a
woman sacrificed at a
Viking ship burial at
Ballyteare, Isle of Man,
Britain. It can be seen
that the top of her head
was chopped off.*

two wolves, Freki and Geri, which he personally fed with gobbets of raw meat. He was one-eyed because he had drunk from the well of the wise god Mimir (*see* Chapter 1), and had willingly surrendered an eye for the continuing wisdom he received.

He was instrumental in starting the war between the Vanir and the Aesir. A witch called Gullveig – probably one of the Vanir – came to Asgard and explained to Odin and the other Aesir that she was consumed by the lust for gold. The Aesir were revolted by her avariciousness, and determined to put her to death; they tried this three times. The Aesir then gave up their attempts and the witch, now called Heid, was permitted to wander Asgard. (There is a possibility that Heid and Freya were really one and the same.) However, the Vanir were enraged when they heard how she had been treated, and soon it was clear that there must be conflict between the two races of gods. The war began when Odin impatiently threw his great spear at the rallied Vanir.

Odin's halls were Gladsheim, Valaskialf and Valhalla; the last of these is discussed later in this book.

The cult of Odin spread far further eastwards than one might have expected. There is no room here to discuss the matter in detail, but it is worth looking at one aspect. There are mentions in the myths of wives being killed, or killing themselves, at the funerals of their warrior husbands – the death of Nanna at the funeral of Balder (*q.v.*) is one example. This seems to have been a regular habit of the Vikings, because double graves have been found in plenty. The practice seems to have diffused eastward across Europe and Asia, and has obvious connections with the Indian ritual of *suttee*. However, as with so many aspects of cultural archaeology, it is almost impossible to work out the directions in which ideas spread.

Odin was simultaneously a wise, a kind and a cruel god, and as such he may represent human nature – for all of us can be simultaneously wise, kind and cruel.

SIF

Not a lot is known about the goddess Sif. She seems to have been a fertility goddess whose prominence had faded by the time the chroniclers were writing their tales. Thor was her second husband; to her first, an anonymous frost giant, she bore a son called Uller. Her sons by Thor were called Magni and Modi.

The reason for guessing that she was connected with fertility is that she had a mane of beautiful golden hair that reached all the way to the ground; this is taken to represent abundant corn. She was extremely proud of her hair, as was Thor, so neither of them were terribly amused when one night as she slept someone came along and cut it all off. When things like that happened in Asgard, the culprit was invariably Loki. Thor responded to the situation with his usual subtlety, and so a few moments later a battered and bloodied Loki discovered that he'd promised that somehow – anyhow – he'd get Sif a new head of hair from somewhere. No, not a wig: it had to be genuine, growing, golden hair.

Such things are not easy to procure, and Loki knew that he had no alternative but to seek aid from the master craftsmen of the nine worlds, the dwarfs of Svartalfaheim. He went to the smithy of a dwarf called Dvalin and persuaded him to make the hair. The dwarf did a miraculous job (literally: the dwarfs could use rune-magic as much as physical skill in their work) and, despite the fact that all Loki offered by way of payment was a string of empty promises, went on to create also Frey's magic ship Skidbladnir and Odin's magic spear Gungnir. Loki was amazed by the magnificence of these gifts and also by the gullibility of the dwarf, who had done so much for so little payment.

He was on his way back to Asgard when a thought struck him. If one dwarf could be so easily duped,

mightn't others be likewise? No sooner thought than tried! Instants later he was showing the three treasures to two dwarfs called Brock and Sindri (in some versions Eitri) and enthusing to them over how, surely, no dwarf could ever hope again to make anything quite as fine – in fact, the god got so carried away that he bet the two dwarfs that, if they could craft anything better, as judged by the gathered Aesir, they could chop off his head! 'All right,' said the dwarfs smugly, and it was at that moment that Loki realized he might have made a mistake.

Sindri told Brock to keep the bellows blowing consistently, without any pause whatsoever, while he himself went off to mutter the appropriate runes. As Brock worked away an insect flew in and landed on his hand, stinging him very painfully, but he didn't miss a beat. When Sindri reappeared they pulled from the forge Gullinbursti, the great magical boar that Frey would use to ride across the sky. The dwarfs set to work making the next artefact. This time while Sindri was out of the smithy chanting the runes the gadfly reappeared and stung Brock on the cheek. Once again, the doughty dwarf managed to keep up the regular pumping of the bellows – although he must have been becoming pretty suspicious about the shape-changer Loki's reputation for honest wagering. And this time the product of the forge was the magical golden ring (or armlet) Draupnir which, every ninth night, would produce eight others identical with itself; in time it was to become the property of Odin.

Loki realized that these two treasures were almost beyond compare and that there was a very good chance that the Aesir might prefer them to the others. This time, as Brock was pumping away, the gadfly stung him on the eyelid, so that blood ran down into the dwarf's eye. Blinded, he took his hand away from the bellows for just a moment to wipe the blood away. The object the two dwarfs then drew from the forge was the mighty hammer Miölnir, which would of course be-

LEFT *Discovered in a tenth-century Swedish Viking grave – Arab coins. Clearly the Viking civilization had contacts far beyond the geographical limits we popularly assume.*

come the property of Thor. It was perfect in every respect except for the fact that its handle was perhaps just a trifle too short.

Loki and the dwarfs went to Asgard with all six of these wonderful gifts. The god was not particularly worried, because of the imperfection of Miölnir. The gifts were handed out to their various recipients, and the Aesir marvelled at all of them. Sif's golden hair, everyone agreed, was if anything more splendid than her previous mane had been. However, they pointed out that Miölnir, wielded by Thor, was the most valuable of all the gifts because it could guard them from the predations of the giants.

The gods laughed as Loki tried to bargain his way out of this one. They were still laughing when he fled from the hall. Brock begged Thor, on the honour of the Aesir, to bring the wizard of lies back so that the wager could be completed, and the huge god recognized the force of this argument. He fetched Loki and placed him in front of the others, and all waited for the execution. However, Loki had been thinking further. His head, it was true, was forfeit to Brock and Sindri, but not his neck: if the dwarfs could find some way of decapitating him without harming his neck then he would be the last to stop them.

The Aesir and the dwarfs realized that, alas, Loki had a point here (shades of *The Merchant of Venice*). But the reason the dwarfs had wanted Loki's head was to stop his mischievous lying. Brock therefore said that he would be content to sew up Loki's lips, and this he did with Sindri's magic awl. The god's agony was excruciating, and he ran from the place screaming as he tore away the thongs. The Aesir laughed all the more merrily at his discomfiture, which was perhaps unwise of them, because thereafter Loki became ever more malicious.

THOR

The god of thunder was among the most important three in the Norse pantheon, the others being Odin (obviously) and Loki. He was responsible for the weather and crops, as well as for sea-voyages that might be affected by the weather. Interestingly, the cracking of the sky during thunderstorms was not regarded with dread by the Norse: instead, they regarded it as a sign that Thor was carrying out his responsibilities, which were, essentially, the slaughter of giants. We can wonder if, perhaps, the Scandinavians equated the crashing of thunder with the equally loud sounds of sintering glaciers, because the frost giants were of course connected with the glaciers that were so much a feature of the northern part of the Viking terrain.

As sophisticated as he was gentle, Thor was red-bearded, gluttonous and loud-voiced: his standard way of dealing with any problem was to kill anyone foolish enough to be nearby. Perhaps for this reason he has been enduringly loved. His most significant manifestation in popular culture during this century being the long-running series of his adventures published in the comics. His invincible hammer was Miölnir and his wife was the beautiful goddess Sif; it is hard to work out which of the two he loved the more, but we can guess it was the hammer. Thor, because of his violent encounter with the giant Hrungnir, will spend all of the rest of time until Ragnarok with a stone implanted in his head.

The tales of Thor's adventures can be found on many pages of this book: the reader is referred to the index. Here are a few not covered elsewhere. The story of Thor and Hrungnir and how the former got a lump of stone in his head clearly demonstrates Thor's approach to things.

It all started when Odin was out on one of his rambles around the world. Astride his eight-legged steed Sleipnir, the father of the gods came to the hall of the giant Hrungnir, generally known to be the strongest of all the giants. It was only moments later that Odin and Hrungnir agreed a wager: Sleipnir versus the giant's horse, Gullfaxi (Golden-mane) – the prize, should Odin lose, being his own head.

Soon the two riders were spurring their steeds into action, and soon after that Odin, realizing that the giant's horse might indeed be the swifter of the two, was galloping very speedily indeed towards Asgard, where he knew Hrungnir could not follow. For his part the giant didn't notice what direction they were taking until he found himself just outside Valhalla – not the best of discoveries, for it was likely to mean that he'd lost his life. The giant was understandably furious about this deception but prepared to meet his doom; luckily the Aesir recognized that he had been rather ill done-by and, instead of killing him, invited him in for a meal.

Mead was swallowed in pints, then quarts, and then gallons; the giant followed this act by consuming whole oceans of mead. Hrungnir began to wax large on his ambition to destroy Asgard and all the gods and goddesses dwelling there, with the exception of Freya and Sif, whom he respected for something other than their minds. This caused the sort of frigid silence most of us have experienced at mortal dinner parties.

And it was at this stage that Thor came back from one of his journeys. He was incensed to discover that Hrungnir was there in the first place, and even more so that the giant was regarding his (Thor's) wife, Sif, with a certain degree of mental impropriety. The god proposed to resolve this little argument by hammering the giant's head down between his shoulderblades. The other Aesir, however, differed: they pointed out that the laws of hospitality forbade random slaughter of guests – especially those who'd had too much to drink, and whose words could therefore not be taken seriously – and so Thor had to bite his tongue as Hrungnir left. The two of them, though, agreed that three days later (by which time Hrungnir would presumably have recovered from his hangover) they would meet for a formal duel at a place called Griottunagard.

The morning after, Hrungnir realized that he had been rather foolish. He consulted some of the other giants as to how he might get out of the duel, and they told him it was impossible. However, they did point out that the formalities of the duel meant that not only did Hrungnir have to do battle with Thor, their two squires had to fight each other: surely it would be easy enough to elect a squire who could make mincemeat out of Thor's squire, Thialfi (see below). This struck Hrungnir as a good idea, and so, not wanting to leave too much to doubt in the contest between the squires, he gave orders that a nine-mile-tall clay giant called Mokerkialfi should be constructed to fight against Thialfi. Into this vast edifice the giants placed a mare's

heart – a human heart would not have been sufficient – but they became nervous when they noticed that even this powerful organ was fluttering with worry.

Hrungnir had become less worried. He was vast and had a shield, club, heart and skull made of stone; his squire was even vaster and, it would seem, twice as invulnerable. The duel proved in fact to be a walkover, because Thialfi had little difficulty in slaughtering Mokerkialfi and Thor even less in killing Hrungnir. However, the giant held up his stone club in an attempt to ward off the thrown hammer of Thor; the club shattered into millions of pieces, which can now be found all over the world as fragments of flint. One of these bits of rock flew into Thor's forehead. At the time it caused the god to collapse forward into unconsciousness, but fortunately his descending hand brought down his hammer, Miölnir, on Hrungnir's head, and —— the giant died as a result.

One of the giant's legs fell over Thor. Luckily the god's son Magni strolled up and – although still aged only three – was able to remove the hugely heavy leg. Thor rewarded his son by giving him the steed Gullfaxi.

And that was the end of that adventure – except for the problem of the shard of stone in Thor's forehead. The Aesir tried everything to get it out, and finally thought they would succeed in doing so when they secured the service of a powerful sorceress called Groa. However, for reasons described in Chapter 1, even this proved of no avail.

Thor had two regular attendants: the boy Thialfi (who became important, as we've seen) and a girl, Roskva. The god gained them in a rather despicable way. He and Loki were wandering the world when the two gods decided that they would like lodging for the night. They took this from a very poor peasant couple, who produced a supper that was in no way big enough to satisfy Thor's huge appetite. The god therefore killed their only two

LEFT *Icelandic bronze statuette, dating from about the year 1000, showing Thor with his hammer.*

goats – although he told the family that, should they leave all the bones untouched and put them back into the empty skins of the animals, things would be all right in the morning. This would have been an honest enough scheme had not Loki encouraged the son of the house, Thialfi, to break one of the bones and lick out its marrow. The next day Thor touched the two heaps of skin and bones with his hammer and suddenly there were two living goats again.

One of them was lame, though, and this made Thor very angry – angry enough to threaten to slaughter the entire family, even though they had given him hospitality for the night. In order to spare all of their lives, the peasant offered Thor Thialfi, the culprit, and his sister Roskva as slaves for eternity. Thor accepted at once.

The gaining of these two slaves occurred during a venture of Thor's to Jotunheim, the land of the giants; the gods had become concerned that the giants were beginning to be too impertinent. Taking the two children with them, Thor and Loki quested on into Jotunheim, their destination a place called Utgard. That night they were cold and lonely, and were only too happy to discover a house where they could sleep; the house was rather strange, but they didn't mind that – all they wanted was somewhere they could sleep. However, sleep was not as easy to come by as they had hoped, because every now and then the ground trembled. Finally the two gods retreated into an annexe of the house, and there at last they were able to sleep in peace.

The reason that the ground had been shaking became obvious to them the following morning when they stumbled, bleary-eyed, out of the strangely shaped house. Nearby a giant was snoring. He almost immediately registered their less than friendly stares and awoke; he reached around him for something that he had lost during the night and soon found it. It was a glove – and also it was the oddly shaped house in which Thor and Loki had spent the night. The annexe which they had finally discovered was the thumb of the glove.

The giant told the two gods that his name was Skrymir; he, too, was on the way to Utgard, and he would gladly show them the way. He offered to share his provisions with them and they readily accepted, because they were running low on supplies. The giant showed what he meant by 'sharing' when he scooped up their pathetically thin bag and simply popped it into his own. All day long the two gods and the two children suffered the tortures of hunger as they did their best to keep up with Skrymir. Things didn't improve that evening, despite the fact that the giant tossed them his bag of provisions: even the mighty Thor was unable to get the damned thing open.

Brought to a pitch of fury by this and by Skrymir's snoring, Thor came as near to rational argument as he usually did. His first piece of witty repartee was to crash Miölnir down on Skrymir's forehead with a mighty blow; the giant responded by half-waking and enquiring if a forest leaf might have landed on his brow. Thor, ever the diplomat, waited until the giant was fast asleep once more: this time he brought his hammer down viciously on the top of Skrymir's skull. Again the giant half-awoke, this time enquiring if, perhaps, an acorn had dropped down onto his head. Questions like these did not please Thor, and so the god kept himself awake, loathing the incessant snoring, until it was nearly dawn. Then he crept across to where Skrymir was sleeping and buried Miölnir up to the very hilt in the giant's brains. The giant stirred and wondered if perhaps a bird seated in a branch above him had shat on his head.

Grey with lack of sleep, Thor roused his companions; the god was treated to a discourse from Skrymir about how he (the giant) was a veritable midget in comparison with the denizens of Utgard. Thor's temper was as sweet as might be imagined.

Thanks to Skrymir's guidance, the four of them were able to make their way to Utgard, which was where the giant Utgard-Loki lived. Rather to their surprise they found themselves welcomed by him, although he did make tactless remarks about their diminutive stature. They were heralded into a hall where countless giants and giantesses were feasting.

A challenge was soon set up between Loki and Utgard-Loki (who was, incidentally, no relation to the god). Loki avowed that he could eat more

swiftly than anyone or anything in the nine worlds. The giant nodded and chuckled, and gave orders that a great trough of food should be set up the length of one of the huge tables. Loki was commanded to start eating at one end and Utgard-Loki's champion, Logi, at the other. To his astonishment Loki discovered that, when he reached the midpoint, his rival had devoured not only the food, as Loki had done, but the trough as well.

Thor felt that the honour of the Aesir had to be retrieved, and so he proposed a second contest. He told Utgard-Loki that there was no one in all the nine worlds who could swig so much mead as he could, and so he would like to suggest a drinking contest. He would drain whatever vessel the company could put in front of him. The giant immediately called for a horn of mead and, on its arrival,

RIGHT *Swedish silver pendant representing Thor's hammer, found in a Viking grave at Öländ believed to date from the tenth or eleventh century.*

explained that in his hall modest drinkers required three draughts to finish it, reasonable tipplers a couple, and real experts only the one. Thor regarded himself as a real expert and so was surprised to find, having taken a draught so huge that he felt his head would explode, that he had hardly reduced the liquid's level at all. A second attempt made very little more difference. A third, and the horn was still almost full. Thor slumped down in defeat.

Thialfi was then asked to race. His opponent was a boy called Hugi. At his first attempt Thialfi was soundly beaten; in later attempts he found Hugi strolling back to ask if he could offer any help.

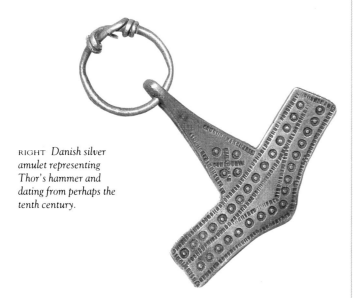

RIGHT *Danish silver amulet representing Thor's hammer and dating from perhaps the tenth century.*

Thor offered to show his huge strength, and the giant laughed. He asked the god to try to lift one of the cats of Utgard, which Thor tried with little success. 'All right,' said the giant, 'if that foe proved too much for you, why not have a try against my old nanny, Elli?' Once again Thor proved humiliatingly incapable of putting up even a decent fight. He and Loki – rather surprisingly, in view of the Aesir's disposition to cheat in these affairs – finally admitted that they had been well and truly beaten by the giant's champions. Utgard-Loki smiled and offered them a bed for the night.

The following morning the giant himself escorted the quartet away from his hall. He had to confess, he said, that in many ways he had cheated them. He had taken on the guise of the huge Skrymir and, while pretending to be asleep, had interposed a mountain between Thor's hammer-blows and himself; otherwise he would have been slain – as it was, all the mountains of the worlds showed the scars of the blows. Loki's opponent in the eating competition, Logi, had in fact been fire, than which nothing can eat faster. Thialfi's opponent in the running race, Hugi, was none other than thought – obviously nobody and nothing can hope to race against the speed of thought. The horn out of which Thor had been drinking had been connected with the wide ocean, which, plainly, even this great god could never hope to drain – although he'd managed, creditably, to cause a noticeable drop in the water level. The cat with which Thor had fought had been Jormungand, the World Serpent, which was well known to be unliftable. When Thor had been wrestling old nurse, Elli, he had had little chance because in fact she was old age: no one can hope successfully to resist old age.

Thor would have liked to have exacted vengeance for all these deceptions, and he started to whirl his hammer in preparation. However, Utgard-Loki wisely disappeared, and the thunder-god was never able thereafter to find the giant's hall.

The thunder-god had various other adventures with giants, often involving Loki. The recovery of his hammer from Thrym involved him disguising himself as Freya (*q.v.*). He destroyed Geirrod and his daughters as well as the previously amicable giant Hymir. In fact, it is curious that any of the giant race should show anything other than loathing for this god, so many of them did he slay, yet there are some examples of them being helpful to him – for example, his life would have been forfeited had it not been for the prior assistance of a giantess called Grid.

LEFT *Stone from
Lärbro, Sweden,
currently in the
Museum of National
Antiquities, Stockholm.
In the central panel we
can see Odin's horse
Sleipnir carrying a dead
hero to Valhalla.*

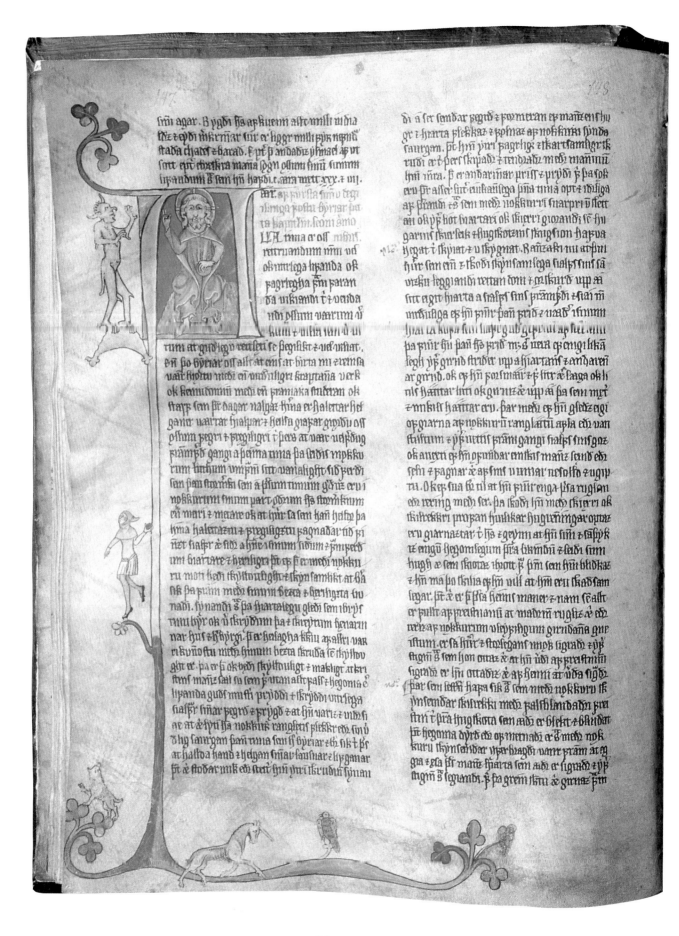

VALI

Vali, the god of eternal light, was conceived with no purpose other than to avenge the death of Balder. A dead prophetess had told Odin that he must mate with the goddess Rind to produce this child, who would grow to adulthood in a single day (quite a number of the lesser deities did this) and then, before he had either washed his face or combed his hair – as the prophetess eloquently put it – slay Hoder; for more details of this prophecy *see* the discussion of Balder earlier in this chapter.

Rind, his mother, is generally taken to have been an earth-goddess. One tale of his conception, possibly tacked on later, portrays her as a mortal – although perhaps, despite her mortal origins, she afterwards became a goddess.

The Rind in this particular tale was the only child of a king called Billing. Her father's country was being threatened by invaders and he was now too old to go to war to repel them, yet she stubbornly refused to take a husband – despite the fact that her beauty had attracted, like iron filings to a magnet, exquisitely handsome suitors from all directions. This was good news for Odin because, in order to avenge the death of Balder, the god had of necessity to sire Vali with Rind. Accordingly, one day Odin, in the guise of a mortal, turned up at Billing's palace offering his services as a military commander. The king, desperate for any help he could get, took him on immediately, and it wasn't very long before the enemies had been repulsed. The triumphant general begged Billing's permission to pay court to his daughter, and there was very little argument. From the father, that is: Rind had other ideas, and sent the grizzled soldier packing.

Odin next appeared as a smith called Rosterus. He could make the most marvellously beautiful brooches and bangles, which delighted all of the court, including Billing and Rind herself. The request for permission to woo being duly granted, the smith tried his luck. The response from Rind was painful to him, to say the least, and he was never seen again at Billing's palace.

The god decided that perhaps middle-aged soldiers and crinkled smiths were not quite what Rind had in mind as a future husband, so next time he turned up as a mighty-thewed warrior – but with the same result. Odin was annoyed at being constantly hit about the head and worse, and so he levelled at her a runestaff, chanting vicious magic spells. Rind collapsed at this onslaught and, by the time she'd revived, the bulky stud had gone. Even after her recovery she was witless. Billing wept for the plight of his daughter, and was much cheered when an old woman arrived at the palace announcing that she alone could bring the lass back to reality. The hag publicly tried a footbath on Rind but without success; there was no other option, she said, but that Rind be put completely under her control. Billing agreed eagerly. Now that this wish had been granted the old woman revealed that in fact she was Odin in disguise. Rind, over whom whom he had been given total mastery, had no choice but to have sex with him – and thereby Vali could be conceived. (The rape theme recurs disturbingly often in the Norse legends.)

An important point about Vali is that he will survive Ragnarok (*see* Chapter 6). He is one of the comparatively few gods who will do so.

Valhalla

Valhalla was the hall of Odin to which the warriors slaughtered in battle – the Einheriar – were brought so that they could enjoy a glorious afterlife. The word 'enjoy' is used cautiously, because few of us now would find much pleasure in the daytime activity of the Einheriar. Each morning they had to dress in their armour and then do combat in the plain before Valhalla, perhaps enjoying the lethal blows they dealt to their fellows but, presumably, suffering over and over again the agonies of the lethal blows that had been dealt by others to themselves. Each evening they were brought back to life, free from any of the mutilations they might have suffered, and came back to Valhalla to engage in feats of consuming limitless food and mead. So much did this 'lifestyle' appeal to the Vikings that, apparently, warriors who had failed to be slain during their active years would fall on their own spears in order to qualify for inclusion among the company of the Einheriar.

The boiled meat they ate came from a huge boar called Saehrimnir, and the supplies were unending because, even though the boar was slaughtered each day by Valhalla's cook, Andhrimnir, it would be reborn in time to be slaughtered again for their next meal. The mead came from the udder of Odin's goat Heidrun, who supplied more than enough for the Einheriar, who drank it from the skulls of their enemies. Presumably an additional delight of Valhalla was that no one ever suffered a hangover, because the quantities of mead drunk by the dead warriors were colossal. The servants at these gargantuan feasts were the Valkyries, sumptuous young women whose favours were, one gathers, readily available to the bold – although at the same time they remained everlastingly virginal.

BELOW *Nineteenth-century book illustration by Gaston Bussière showing a highly romanticised image of a valkyrie. In the original legends the valkyries might be beautiful and free* *with their favours once dead warriors had reached Valhalla, but on the battlefield they were regarded as possessed of the utmost sadistic bloodthirstiness.*

RIGHT *A romanticised vision from a nineteenth-century book of the valkyries carrying off slain heroes to Valhalla. The lowermost hero appears to have attracted the attention of a nubile valkyrie through having incurred a fatal hangover.*

RIGHT *Figures in silver from Swedish Viking graves. The one on the right, dating from an eleventh-century grave, shows a stereotyped valkyrie holding up a drinking horn. The one on the left, dating from the previous century, shows a horseman — presumably the warrior himself riding to Valhalla.*

Our modern image of the Valkyries has been coloured by performances of the operas of Richard Wagner: we think of them as objects of ridicule, buxom and garbed in a costume which goes largely unnoticed except for their precarious metal brassières. In fact, according to the Norse, they were far from that. They were beautiful and desirable, yes, and they were also unbelievably sadistic – except to the Einheriar. Assistants to Tyr, the god of war, they rode on their panting steeds – sometimes wolves – across the skies above battlefields, swooping to pluck the dead from the ground and bring them to Valhalla. Sometimes they took monstrous forms and poured rains of blood down over the land or rowed a ship across the skies through a torrent of blood. In one account they are described as seated on a battlefield weaving a tapestry from human intestines, using an arrow for a shuttle and men's heads to weigh down the ends of their gory cords.

Valkyries are connected with several of the heroes, whose wives they became. There is a great deal of evidence that the myth of their existence had some basis in reality (or perhaps the myth gave rise to the reality), and that priestesses did indeed attend Teutonic armies, including the Norse, with the responsibility of, after a battle, selecting those prisoners to be killed and choosing the manner of their death. This latter was generally not pleasant, but could be regarded as an honour conveyed by the victors upon the vanquished. One delightful tribute the Norse made to those who had been bested in battle, but who were regarded as particularly valiant foes, was the Eagle. The prisoner was held face-downwards and split open along the backbone. His ribs were then splayed outwards and his lungs dragged away to form a canopy over them. It was regarded as a particular sign of valour if the victim showed no sign of pain during all this.

FOUR

Tales of the Valkyries

LEFT *Nineteenth-century book illustration showing Brunhild with Gunnar.*

BRUNHILD

The tale of Brunhild is a very muddled one, with several mutually incompatible strands. We shall pick our way through it as best we can.

After the hero Sigurd (*q.v.*) had stolen Fafnir's gold (*see* Chapter 1) he rode on until he came to a hall set high on a mountain. Inside it there was a beautiful woman asleep, dressed in full armour. Instinctively knowing what to do in such circumstances, Sigurd took his sword and cut away her armour, at which point she awoke and told him that her name was Brunhild and that she was a Valkyrie.

This is where the tale starts to become confused. According to the Prose Edda, Sigurd then continued on his way as if nothing had happened until he came to the palace of a king called Giuki, one of whose daughters was Gudrun (*q.v.*). (There is a version that states that Sigurd had agreed to marry Brunhild but that, after he had come to Giuki's court, Queen Grimhild determined that he should marry her daughter and so used magic to erase all memory of his earlier betrothal.) Sigurd married Gudrun and became the blood-brother of two of Giuki's sons, Gunnar and Högni. Sigurd and the two brothers went to ask a king of the Huns called Atli if he would consent to the marriage of his sister Brunhild to Gunnar. (You were forewarned that this would be difficult to unravel.) This sister lived in a hall called Hindarfiall which was surrounded by a curtain of flame; it was well known that she would not consider marriage to any man who was not prepared to ride through the flame. Gunnar's horse refused the challenge, but then Sigurd had a ready answer: he would take the shape of Gunnar and, on his own much braver steed called Grani, endure the fire to capture the hand of Brunhild on Gunnar's behalf. This he did with little difficulty. The beautiful maid took one look at him and was much in love. Sigurd, however, being an honourable man, although he slept with Brunhild did not make love with her – a fact which she must have found rather perplexing. In the morning Sigurd gave her as a wedding gift the ring that Loki had taken as part of Andvari's gold: bearing in mind that this ring was accursed, the wedding gift might perhaps have been better chosen. Then Sigurd rode back to join the two brothers and exchanged forms with Gunnar, who thereafter became Brunhild's loving husband.

There was a certain degree of tension between Brunhild and Gudrun, because both of them were essentially in love with the same man. In one instance the two of them were washing their hair in the river and conducting a boasting contest about the prowess

RIGHT *A carving on a cart recovered from a ninth-century ship burial at Vestfold, Norway, shows on the left how Gunnar met his end. He was condemned by Atli to be cast into a pit of snakes. In the pit, his hands being bound, he played on his harp using his toes, and thereby reduced all but one of the serpents to tranquility. This last serpent – Atli's mother in disguise – gave the fatal bite.*

of their respective husbands. Brunhild bragged about Gunnar's bravery in riding through the wall of flame, and Gudrun broke it to her that the man who had performed this feat had in fact been Sigurd.

Brunhild was not at all delighted to hear this news, and decided that Sigurd's deception should be avenged. She tried to persuade the brothers Gunnar and Högni to kill Sigurd, but they refused, delegating the task instead to their brother Guttorm. Guttorm lost his life while killing Sigurd and Sigurd's infant son; as Gudrun expressed her grief Brunhild laughed mockingly. Soon, however, Brunhild changed her mind: she killed herself in order to be placed on Sigurd's funeral pyre.

There are many variant versions of this story. According to some, Brunhild and Sigurd did not behave quite as decorously as described above when Sigurd had come into Hindarfiall, the result being a daughter called Auslag. The child was still very young when her parents died and so was looked after by her grandfather, Giuki. However, a revolution drove him from his kingdom and he was forced to wander the world as a minstrel, bearing a harp in which was hidden his lovely granddaughter. In the end he was murdered by peasants who thought that there was gold in his harp and who were very disappointed to discover the girl-child. Because they thought she was a deaf-mute they reared her as a skivvy, not noticing that she was growing up to be an exceptionally fair young woman. At last a Viking called Ragnar Lodbrog saw her and fell in love. He had to travel away for a year, killing people in order to attain glory, but when he returned he took her as his bride – and so she became the queen of Denmark.

Another possible interpretation of the story is that Brunhild was initially a mortal. Sigurd, on his death, was clearly destined to be taken to Valhalla. Her love for him was so great that she wished to follow him there, becoming a Valkyrie – and the only

RIGHT *Another rendition of Gunnar in the pit of snakes, this time from a tenth-century Viking–Christian cross at Andreas, Isle of Man, Britain.*

95

RIGHT *An
illustration from FL
Spence's* Rhine
Legends *(1915)
showing Odin and
Brunhild.*

way that she could do this was to kill herself and be consumed beside him on his pyre. Yet another version of her story describes her as a king's daughter rudely plucked by Odin from the mortal world to become the leader of all the Valkyries, a position of honour that meant she became, in effect, Odin's own daughter. Obviously there is always the possibility that these legends are confusing two quite different Brunhilds, one a mortal and the other a Valkyrie. The variation of the tale rendered in Wagner's *Ring* cycle is a far later version, bearing little relation to the Norse legends.

GUDRUN

As with Brunhild, the tales of Gudrun are very confused: it is likely that they are confabulations of legends about two quite separate Gudruns, one a mortal and the other a Valkyrie. The exploits of the 'mortal Gudrun' are discussed above: she was the wife of Sigurd and, as such, was probably less poorly treated in the legends than might have been expected of the Norse, who attributed to women a great many powers and guiles, few of which were very flatteringly portrayed. Like Brunhild, Gudrun may have started off as a mortal and then been transformed into a Valkyrie.

The son of Sigmund and Borghild was called Helgi, and he was a very brave warrior. Gudrun, as she swooped over a battlefield where Helgi and Sinfiotli were fighting with the Hundings, was much taken by the young man. She accordingly descended to Earth and threw herself before him, offering her all. Helgi thanked her but, as it were, he had this battle to fight first: they could be betrothed but the consummation would have to wait a while. After the battle there was only one of the Hundings still standing – a youth called Dag, who was given his freedom on the condition that he would not

seek to carry on the vendetta any longer. Dag agreed to this but then betrayed his oath and slew Helgi.

Gudrun's grief was great; not surprisingly, she laid a curse on Dag. She discovered that the dead Helgi, buried in his mound, was calling for her incessantly, and so she went to him. She found that he was still bleeding prodigiously, and he told her that this was because of her continuing grief: every time she shed a tear, he shed a matching drop of blood. From then on she kept back her tears.

BELOW *Viking period gilt brooch found in a Viking grave in Sweden. It dates from around the ninth and eleventh centuries* AD.

The loving couple were soon reunited. Helgi was gathered to Valhalla and Gudrun joined him there. He became a leader of the armies of the dead warriors, the Einheriar; she, in order to help him, returned to her role as a Valkyrie so that she could bring as many slain warriors as possible to swell the ranks of his armies.

The rest of the tale of the 'mortal Gudrun' is less edifying. While Brunhild had so graphically displayed her love for Sigurd by immolating herself upon his pyre, Gudrun was not prepared to do likewise, so she and her daughter Swanhild fled to the court of a king called Elf. His queen was Thora, and

RIGHT *Arthur Rackham's typically romantic image of Brunhild. Warlike the valkyries might be, but there is little to make us believe that the Vikings saw them as beautiful, clean-limbed maidens like this, rather, they were hideous creatures, akin to vampires or the Irish tripartite death-goddess The Morrigan, when they visited earthly battlefields to carry off the souls of the dead.*

FAR RIGHT *Detail of a cross slab found at Michael, Isle of Man, Britain, dating from the late tenth or early eleventh century; the slab is called 'Joalf's Slab'. The Viking depicted is bearing a spear and a round shield.*

RIGHT *A detail from a stone-carved cross, from Middleton, North Yorkshire, Britain, dating from about the tenth century, showing a Norse warrior laid out for burial. The cross was, of course, a Christian artefact, the burial a pagan one. This mixture of paganism with Christianity became increasingly a characteristic of the late Viking period, until eventually the new religion took over almost completely.*

soon Gudrun and Thora were close friends. However, this situation didn't last too long, because Atli, king of the Huns, was demanding to be avenged upon Gunnar; the latter, now king, was eager to avoid war and so he told Atli that he could marry his sister Gudrun. The marriage was eventually performed, much to Gudrun's disgust: she loathed Atli. In due course she murdered the sons he had sired upon her and served bits of them up to him in a banquet: their skulls were used for goblets, their blood was mixed into the wine, and the meat was their roasted hearts. Then Gudrun revealed the truth to Atli before setting fire to his palace and dying with him and his cronies in the flames.

Swanhild, Gudrun's daughter, met an equally unsavoury end. A king called Ermenrich wanted her as a wife and sent his son Randwer to fetch her. When they reached Ermenrich's palace, however, a lying and treacherous servant called Sibich claimed that, during the journey, Randwer had seduced Swanhild. At Ermenrich's order Randwer was hanged and Swanhild sentenced to be trampled to death by wild horses. Early attempts to carry out this execution failed because of Swanhild's exquisite beauty: the horses simply refused to harm her. In the end she was covered with a blanket to shield her beauty from the horses, and so she lost her life.

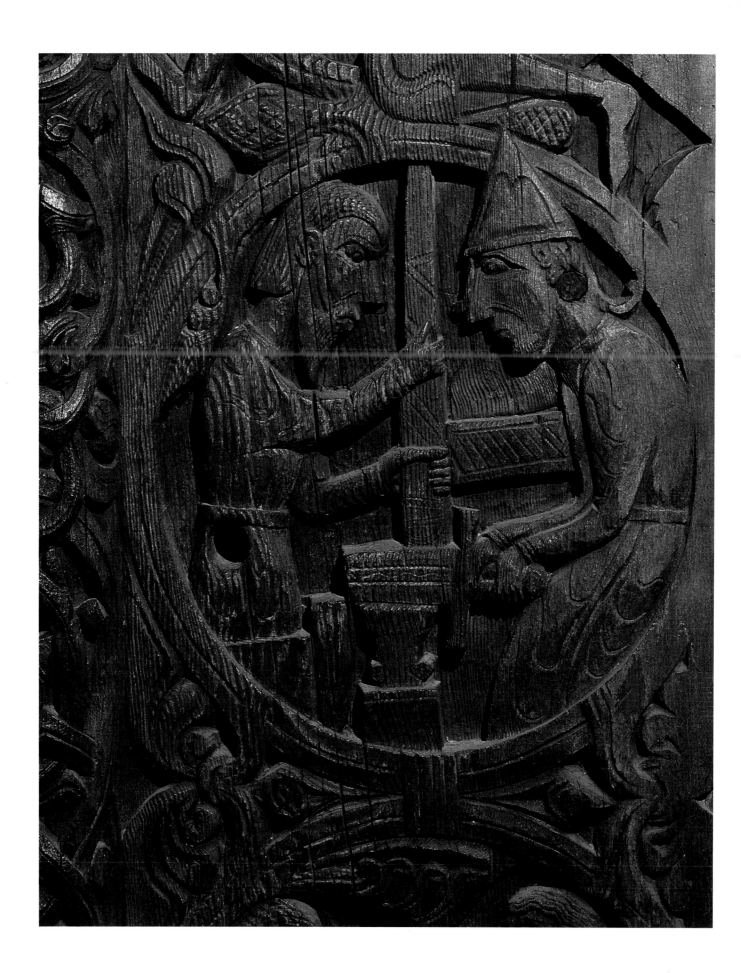

FIVE

Tales of Heroes

LEFT *Detail from a*
twelfth- or thirteenth-
century wooden portal
at Hylestad Church,
Norway, showing the
dwarf Regin reforging
the sword Sigurd had
been given by his father.

FRITHIOF

Frithiof was the son of Thorsten (*q.v.*) and Ingeborg. Early in his life he was given out to a man called Hilding for fostering (this was a not uncommon practice among the Vikings). Hilding later became the foster-father of a girl who was also called Ingeborg; she was the daughter of Thorsten's great friend King Belé. The two children grew up together and, predictably, fell in love with each other; but Hilding forbade them to marry, pointing out that Ingeborg was a princess while Frithiof was merely the son of a hero. Frithiof took this as well as might be expected – in other words, not very.

Belé's heirs were his sons Halfdan and Helgé, neither of whom were particularly popular; Frithiof, on the other hand, was very popular indeed – even with Belé himself. After Halfdan and Helgé had taken over the throne from their father, Frithiof decided to retire from public life, although he pined for Ingeborg.

One Spring, however, Halfdan and Helgé came to visit him and they brought with them their sister. Ingeborg and Frithiof were instantly, once again, madly and passionately in love. After the royal party had left, Frithiof decided to pluck up his courage and follow them in order to beg the two kings, his former playmates, to let him marry their sister. When he came to them, sitting on their father's barrow, Helgé told him that he was not good enough for Ingeborg, being only a peasant's son; he could, however, if he wanted, become one of Helgé's bondsmen. Aroused to a level beyond mere tetchiness, Frithiof drew his sword and sliced Helgé's shield in two. Then he went home, much disgruntled.

Ingeborg was beautiful, and the news of this spread widely, so that princely suitors sent messengers from many lands. One of these was a king called Sigurd Ring, a widower of great age. Ingeborg having, of course, no voice in any of these discussions, Helgé asked various seers and seeresses whether or not there was any chance that the marriage would be successful; Halfdan, more relevantly, wondered if the old man, Sigurd Ring, would be able to – um – give Ingeborg the full joys of marriage. The limp joke came to the ears of Sigurd Ring, who became enraged and announced publicly that he planned to wage war on Halfdan and Helgé. The response of the two kings was less than heroic: they instantly sent Hilding to ask Frithiof to command their armies in an endeavour to repel the threat. Frithiof's reply was that he had been so offended by their earlier remarks that he had little interest in sorting things out for them. Halfdan and Helgé decided that their best course of action was to give in to Sigurd Ring and to give him the hand of their sister, Ingeborg.

Frithiof was not quite so sure that that was the end of the story. He discovered that Ingeborg was pining in a religious house devoted to Balder, and so he went there. It was taboo to speak in this place, but they spoke anyway, and over many days, knowing that Ingeborg's brothers were away. The brothers returned, though; to Frithiof's request that they might think about his offer to lead their armies against Sigurd Ring the two of them – notably Helgé – remarked that they were much more interested in whether or not Frithiof and Ingeborg had been talking with each other in the grove (or monastery) devoted to Balder. Helgé pressed the question: had Frithiof and Ingeborg spoken with each other? There was a long silence before Frithiof replied that, yes, he had.

His sentence was banishment. Ingeborg declined to follow him to the sunny lands he knew lay to the south; she reckoned that now her father was dead she ought to do what her brothers told her.

Helgé was not content with Frithiof's sentence of banishment: he wanted the man dead. The king there-

fore summoned up a couple of witches and asked them to send a storm out to sea so that Frithiof's ship, and all on board her, should be sunk. The witches did their best, but Frithiof, chanting a merry lay, dissuaded the elements from killing him and his crew. In this way they all came to the Orkney Islands. The natives were not much pleased by this, obviously, but Frithiof defeated the berserker, Atlé, whom they sent to challenge him. Frithiof also made friends, in due course, with the king of the Orkneys, Angantyr.

After many months Frithiof came home, only to discover that his hall had been burnt to the ground on the orders of Helgé. Also, he was given the news by Hilding that Ingeborg had been married to Sigurd Ring. He carried out various acts of slaughter and then set sail for Greece, where he lived for some years. He finally returned to the court of Sigurd Ring in the guise of a beggar, a role that he maintained only as long as it took for him to kill one of the courtiers. Sigurd Ring, very decently, did not have him executed

for this crime but instead asked him to doff his disguise; this Frithiof did, thereby meeting the appealing eye of Ingeborg. The hero then had too much to drink, watched with approval by Sigurd Ring. The two men became great friends, and that was the end, for a while, of Frithiof's lust for Ingeborg.

Sigurd Ring died, and at last Frithiof and Ingeborg were free to marry. Helgé accidentally killed himself. Halfdan, on the other hand, swore an oath of friendship with Frithiof, and the two men remained friends until the end of their lives.

SIGMUND

S igmund was the twin brother of the beautiful woman Signy; they were the last two children of Volsung. Sigmund was the only one of all the brothers to realize that Signy didn't want to marry Siggeir, the king of the Goths; however, Odin had a similar idea and turned up for the wedding feast, throwing a sword into the heart of the Branstock, a great oak that grew up through Volsung's hall; according to Odin, whoever was able to remove the sword would become a great hero.

Siggeir, the recent groom, tried to pull the sword from the tree but without success; Volsung was no luckier. Then Sigmund's nine elder brothers had a try, all of them unsuccessfully. Finally Sigmund himself had a go, and the sword immediately slid out of its wooden scabbard; the comparison with King Arthur is very obvious.

King Siggeir offered to buy the weapon but Sigmund refused; it was at this point that the king determined to exterminate Sigmund and all of his kin, including Signy. As Siggeir slept, Signy told Volsung that her new husband was up to no good, but Volsung wouldn't believe her. A while later Volsung sent a fleet of vessels to Siggeir's kingdom; he and all of his war-

LEFT *Reconstruction of a Viking helmet found at Middleton Cross, Yorkshire, Britain.*

riors were murdered. Sigmund himself was lucky enough to escape, although he had to give up his magical sword; he and his brothers were then sentenced to death. Signy was distraught at this, and asked that the death penalty be rescinded; the result was that their sentence was commuted to being tied up to trees in the forest, there to be eaten by wild animals, while Signy was locked up in Siggeir's palace. All of the brothers died except Sigmund; this was because Signy had the idea of smearing honey on his face, so that the wild creatures of the forest licked this away rather than eating him. The beast that attacked him that night attempted a french kiss, thrusting its tongue into Sigmund's mouth; he bit back forcefully, killing it.

Signy arrived to rejoice about her brother's survival; he, for his part, went off to become a smith, operating out of a remote part of the forest.

That wasn't the end of the story, though. Signy concluded that the sons she bore by Siggeir were wimps and decided to send them to Sigmund for a bit of bracing. The test to which he put them was to knead some bread and not notice that, within the dough, there was a viper. The first son of Signy either noticed it and fled or was killed by Sigmund; the second got the same treatment. Signy despaired of the third son she might have by Siggeir, and so she decided to have one by Sigmund instead; she called on a beautiful witch, adopted her form, and slept with her brother. The resulting son was Sinfiotli. He showed himself to be better than his stepbrothers because, when baking bread, he simply baked the viper along with all the rest.

Sigmund and Sinfiotli became boon companions and soon began to rush around Scandinavia killing people, in the typical manner of heroes. In one of their adventures they became werewolves. They discovered two men sleeping and, on the wall, a pair of wolfskins. Father and son immediately donned these, wondering what it would feel like. Moments later they were werewolves that ran through the forest and ate anyone who came in their way. The two got so excited that they started to fight each other; Sigmund killed Sinfiotli. The father then watched as two weasels fought with each other; one killed the other but then restored it to life by laying on its breast a particular leaf; Sigmund followed suit and brought his son Sinfiotli back to life. The two of them realized that they'd been a bit stupid risking their lives as werewolves, and so as soon as possible they shed their skins and reverted to human form.

Sigmund and Sinfiotli now decided that they would exact their revenge on Siggeir. They went to Siggeir's hall, where they were soon discovered by two of Signy's youngest children; their mother told Sigmund to cut off the children's heads but he refused, so she did it herself.

Sigmund and Sinfiotli were captured and sentenced to death by Siggeir; their punishment was that they should be buried alive in a mound, separated by a wall. The mound was almost complete when Signy came along and threw at Sinfiotli's feet a bale of hay. He assumed that it might contain a loaf of bread, but actually it contained Sigmund's magical sword; as quick as thought Sinfiotli hacked an exit from the burial tomb.

The two heroes immediately rushed back to Volsung's hall and built up a great pile of straw all around it. They set fire to this and then stood at the gate refusing to let anyone escape but the women. An exception was Signy, whom they would have allowed out; she apparently preferred to burn alive as a penance for her infanticide and incestuous adultery.

Sigmund went on to marry the fair princess Borghild and then the equally fair princess Hiordis. Unfortunately a certain King Lygni likewise wanted to marry Hiordis; when Sigmund became the successful suitor Lygni raised an army. In the ensuing war Sigmund slew hundreds but was eventually killed himself.

Sigmund's son was the hero Sigurd (q.v.).

SIGURD

H iordis was pregnant when her husband Sigmund (*q.v.*) was slain. She was lucky enough, however, to meet up with a benevolent Viking called Elf, who asked her to marry him and promised to look after her forthcoming child as if he were its real father. The child arrived and Elf gave him the name Sigurd. In the Germanic version of the legends Sigurd was called Siegfried.

Sigurd's education was entrusted to an infinitely wise man called Regin, and so the boy learned considerable wisdom – music, diplomacy, the carving of runes, smithery, warfare, etc. On attaining adulthood Sigurd was given permission to choose from his stepfather's stable any warhorse he would like. On his way to make the selection Sigurd was met by Odin, who told him that the best means of choice was to drive all of Elf's horses into a nearby river and then pick the one that retained its feet the best in the current. This Sigurd did, and as a result he gained the horse Greyfell, a descendant of Odin's horse Sleipnir.

One day Regin told him of the cursed treasure of Andvari, now guarded by the dragon Fafnir (*see* Chapter 1), and asked him if he would be willing to do battle with Fafnir in order to recover the gold and avenge the crime. Sigurd agreed, and so Regin set out to forge for him an invincible sword. His first two attempts were unsuccessful, Sigurd being able to shatter the swords by crashing them down on an anvil. Then Sigurd remembered the sword of his father, Sigmund, the fragments of which were still kept by Hiordis. From those fragments was forged a mighty blade that, when crashed down on the anvil, made great gouges in it. Regin and Sigurd then set sail for the land of the Volsungs. On the way they picked up Odin, although they didn't realize who this stranger was.

RIGHT *As Regin sleeps, Sigurd roasts the heart of the dwarfish smith's brother, who became the dragon Fafnir. This is a detail from a twelfth- or thirteenth-century carved wooden portal at Hylestad Church in Norway.*

106

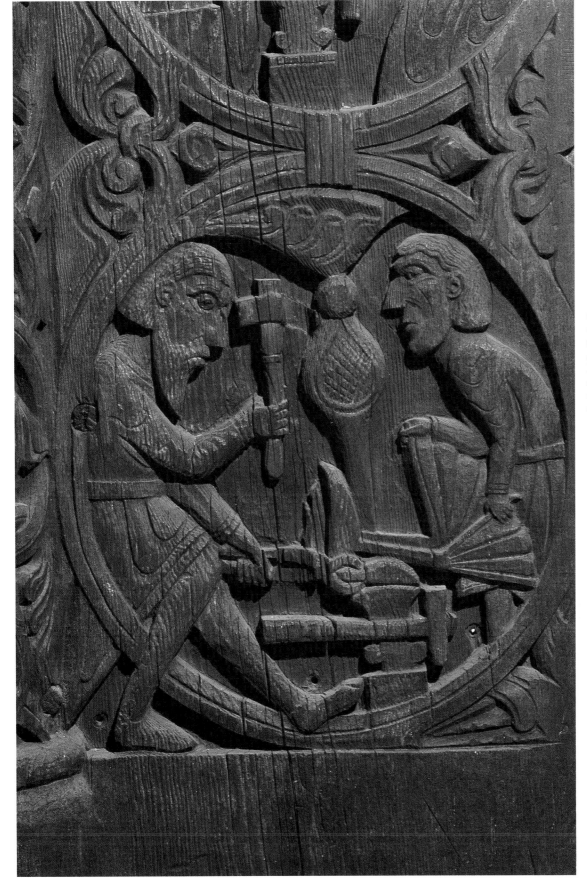

LEFT *Details from a twelfth- or thirteenth- century wooden portal at Hylestad Church, Norway, showing the dwarf Regin reforging the sword Sigurd had been given by his father.*

RIGHT *Part of a Viking cross found at Andreas, Isle of Man, Britain. At top left we can see Sigurd roasting Fafnir's heart.*

BELOW RIGHT *The 'Waterfall of the Gods' in Iceland. According to legend, Thorsten, on being converted to Christianity about AD 1000, threw his pagon idols over these falls.*

Sigurd killed Lygni, the killer of his father, and then moved on, with Regin, to kill Fafnir. Again Odin helped him, this time pointing out that the dragon daily used the same path in order to quench his thirst at a nearby river: all that Sigurd had to do was to lie in wait. The operation was a complete success. Regin asked Sigurd to cut out the dragon's heart, barbecue it and serve it up as a meal, and Sigurd immediately agreed to the request. During the roasting Sigurd at one stage touched the heart with his fingers to see if it were ready yet; the hot meat stung his fingers, and he put them to his lips, immediately finding that he could understand the talk of the birds. They were saying to each other that Regin planned to kill him, and that he would be best advised to kill the sage at once and himself devour the dragon's heart and blood, then to claim the treasure. This Sigurd did. He then awoke Brunhild (*q.v.*) from her timeless sleep and became her betrothed. Unfortunately, he then became enamoured of Gudrun (*q.v.*), a daughter of the king of the Nibelungs, and forgot all about Brunhild. Sigurd had kept some of Fafnir's heart, and at his wedding to Gudrun he gave her a little to eat; he also became a blood-brother of her brothers Gunnar and Högni. Gunnar determined to marry Brunhild, with the results seen in Chapter 4. Guttorm, the third son of the king of the Nibelungs, was deputed to slay Sigurd, and succeeded, although he lost his own life in doing so. Brunhild shared her one-time lover's funeral pyre.

THORSTEN

Thorsten was one of the nine sons of the hero Viking (*q.v.*) by his second marriage and a survivor of the war with the sons of Viking's great friend Njorfe. The war started when one of Njorfe's sons, during a game of ball, treacherously hit out at one of Viking's sons, who later killed him.

Thorsten became a pirate. He encountered one of the two surviving sons of Njorfe, Jokul, who seems to have been a rather unpleasant piece of work: he had killed the king of Sogn, banished the kingdom's prince, Belé, and turned the princess Ingeborg into an old hag. Jokul used evil magic in attempts to kill Thorsten, but was unsuccessful – in large part thanks to the help of the seeming hag, whom Thorsten agreed to marry in thanks for her assistance. The hero restored Belé to his rightful throne and was delighted to discover that Ingeborg was in fact a beautiful young maiden.

Thorsten, Belé and another hero called Angantyr had many adventures together. They recovered a ship called Ellida that had once been given to Viking by the god Aegir (*q.v.*). They conquered the Orkney Isles, of which Angantyr became the king, although he pledged himself to pay an annual tribute to Belé. Then Thorsten and Belé regained from a pirate called Soté a magic arm-ring that had been forged by Völund (*q.v.*).

Thorsten and Ingeborg had a son called Frithiof (*q.v.*), who himself became a hero.

VIKING

Viking was a grandson of a Norwegian king called Haloge; according to some versions of the mythology Haloge was in fact the god Loki. Whatever the truth of this, Viking was born on an island called Bornholm, in the Baltic Sea. By the time he had reached the age of 15 he was so strong and huge that rumours of him reached Sweden and in particular a princess called Hunvor. At the time Hunvor was being pestered by the attentions of a giant. Pausing only to collect from his father a magic sword called Angurvadel, Viking sailed to Sweden and did battle with the giant. He would have married Hunvor there and then but it was considered that he was too young. He therefore sailed around the North Sea for some years, being tormented by the relatives of the dead

In the whalebone carvings on the early-eighth-century Franks Casket, now in the British Museum, we find a delicious mix of Norse and Christian mythologies. RIGHT *In this section we see, on the left, Völund's smithy and, on the right, the Adoration of the Magi.*

giant and befriended by a man called Halfdan; in due course Viking married Hunvor and Halfdan married a servant of hers called Ingeborg.

Over the next few years Viking and Halfdan led raids to other countries during which they took great pleasure in slaughtering, preferably females whom they first raped. Nevertheless, they were faithful to their wives; such is the way of Norse mythology. They also made friends, after a long war, with a king called Njorfe.

Hunvor died; Viking put out their son Ring to a foster-father and then remarried. He and his new wife had nine sons; Njorfe and *his* wife had the same number. Despite the fact that their fathers had sworn all the oaths of friendship, the sons sustained a long-term antagonism between the two families. Much of the time this took an innocent enough form: as far as one can work out from the legends, the two sets of lads merely met each other on the Norse equivalent of a

football pitch. However, one of Njorfe's sons committed an overly 'cynical' foul on one of Viking's sons, so the latter killed him. This murder infuriated Viking, and thus he banished the boy; the other brothers told their father that they would follow him into exile. The eldest of these sons was Thorsten; to him Viking gave the sword Angurvadel.

Njorfe's sons were not satisfied by this, and followed Viking's sons into the faraway land where they hid. There was a great battle, with the result that only two of Viking's sons – Thorsten and Thorer – and two of Njorfe's sons – Jokul and another – survived. These two pairs swore undying hatred for each other, so Viking sent his own two sons to the court of Halfdan. Thorsten had adventures of his own, during one of which he killed Jokul.

VÖLUND

Völund is well known as Wayland or Weland the Smith; under the former name he turns up, for example, as a character in Walter Scott's novel *Kenilworth* (1821). His brothers were called Egil and Slagfinn.

One day the three brothers came across three Valkyries – Alvit, Olrun and Svanhvit – swimming in a river, and immediately raped them, having stolen the Valkyries' swan plumage so that they were no longer able to leave the Earth. For nine years the three maidens remained with their captors, but then they were able to recover their plumage and return to Valhalla. This was much mourned by the three brothers, and Egil and Slagfinn set off on a quest to see if they could rediscover their brides. Völund, however, reckoned that their search was futile, and so stayed at home.

Alvit had given him a ring, and he looked on this lovingly. A practised smith, he made 700 other rings exactly like it and tied all 701 of them up in a bundle. One day he discovered that one of the rings had been stolen and he was much cheered, believing that this meant that Alvit had returned to Earth to reclaim it and would soon come back to be his wife again.

That night, however, he was attacked and taken prisoner by the king of Sweden, Nidud, who had confiscated Alvit's ring (giving it to his daughter Bodvild) as well as Völund's magic sword. The hapless smith was incarcerated on an island, his hamstrings being cut so that he could have no hope of escape. There he was forced to labour each and every day at his forge to manufacture weapons and ornaments for the brutal king. Völund's opinion of Nidud was by this time not of the highest, and all the time he plotted escape and revenge. He made himself a pair of wings just like those Alvit had used, so that he could fly to join her in Valhalla.

Nidud brought to Völund one day the smith's magic sword, asking for it to be repaired. Völund pretended to comply, but in fact hid it and returned to Nidud an exact replica. A little afterwards he lured Nidud's sons into his smithy, slaughtered them, used their skulls to make goblets and their teeth and eyes as adornments; these he gave to the royal couple, who received them as precious gifts, little realizing their origins. Having exacted his next revenge by raping Bodvild and repossessing from her his magic ring, he donned the wings he had crafted and flew to Nidud's palace, where he enumerated loudly and at length the king's failings and sins. Nidud called for Völund's brother Egil, who was now his slave, and instructed him to shoot Völund down out of the sky; however, Völund signalled to his brother to aim his arrow at a bladder he clutched that was full of the blood of Nidud's sons. This Egil did, and Nidud assumed that his royal archer had slain the enemy, little realizing that Völund had flown.

Völund then rejoined Alvit and is still living with her and practising his craft: he will continue to do so until Ragnarok.

RIGHT *Made from walrus ivory around 1135–1150 and found on the Isle of Lewis, Scotland, this rook ('castle') comes from a Viking chess set. When we think of the Vikings we envisage only mindless slaughter, but in fact they regarded chess as such a fine sport that it could have been their equivalent of football.*

SIX

Ragnarok

In this book we have concentrated to exclusion on things that have already happened – or, at least, have done so according to the Norse myths. However, the mythology encompassed also what was going to happen at some unspecified time in the future, when the gods themselves would die. Here there is a definite parallel with the Christian account, in Revelation, of the forthcoming Apocalypse, for Ragnarok too is a final battle between the forces of good and evil. A major difference is that after Ragnarok, unlike after the Apocalypse, there will be a rebirth of both a new pantheon and all life on Earth. The German equivalent of Ragnarok is, of course, Götterdämmerung.

LEFT *Swedish bronze matrix, dating from about the eighth century, used for fashioning plaques for Viking helmets: a man with a boar on either side. Could this represent an early version of Odin with his two wolves? Or could it symbolize the last deathly struggle at Ragnarok between Odin and Fenris?*

What will happen at this terrible time? The first answer to the question is that the popular translation of Ragnarok as the 'twilight of the gods' is false: this is to be the *death* of the gods. It will be brought about largely because the gods tolerated the existence of the evil Loki, who, bound in the most horrific circumstances, has for long plotted their downfall.

The first sign of the onset of Ragnarok will be Fimbulvetr, a years-long savage winter when snow will constantly fall from all points of the compass. The wolves chasing the Sun and the Moon will catch up with them and devour them. Loki and Fenris, as well as Hel's dog, Garm, will succeed in breaking their bonds in order to attack the gods. Nidhug, the dragon gnawing at one of the roots of Yggdrasil, will at last succeed in severing it. The god Heimdall (*q.v.*) will sound a note on his trumpet, warning of what is imminent, and this note will be heard by all. The Aesir and the Einheriar (the dead warriors taken to Valhalla from the battlefield) will hear this blast and rally to Vigrid, where the final battle will take place. The seas will be stirred up into a frenzy, and this will trigger Jormungand, the World Serpent, into raising himself from his bed in the depths of the ocean to join in the battle.

The serpent's writhing will create huge waves, and one of these will launch a ship called Naglfari, created entirely from the nails of those of the dead whose kin have failed to cut their nails. Loki will board this ship, accompanied by a horde from the realm of Muspell. The frost giants, too, will sail in a ship to Vigrid in order to battle with the Aesir; their captain will be the giant Hrym. Hel will join the forces of evil, as will her sycophants Garm and Nidhug. Surtr, the flame giant, will come to add to Loki's army, followed by numerous of his kin. As this last army rides over Bifrost its sheer weight will shatter the rainbow bridge.

The gods will show no fear despite the strength of the armies facing them. Odin will, one last time, consult the

LEFT *Part of the Gosforth Cross, showing one of the events of Ragnarok: Odin is attacked by a winged dragon.*

RIGHT *The seeress who told Odin that Ragnarok was inevitable during his sojourn into the realm of Hel is seen at the upper left of this section of a cross slab found at Jurby, Isle of Man, Britain, which dates from the tenth century.*

Norns and Mimir, and then rejoin his fellows. Then the battle will be joined.

Odin will be slain in his duel with Fenris. Surtr will kill Frey and Loki Heimdall. Tyr will die at the teeth of Garm, and Thor in a torrent of venom from the mouth of Jormungand. Vidar will tear Fenris to pieces. Surtr will set fire to Yggdrasil, thereby destroying also the halls of the gods and all of the plant-life of the Earth.

RIGHT *Three faces of the tenth-century Gosforth Cross depict scenes from Viking mythology, especially Ragnarok. The fourth (eastern) face contains an image of the Crucifixion, showing how the two mythologies had blended by this early stage.*

However, things will come into being again. A daughter of Sol will drive the chariot of the Sun, and will do so in a much better fashion than her mother had done. The first two mortals of the new race after Ragnarok will be called Lif and Lifthrasir; she and he will repopulate the Earth with their children. The gods Vali and Vidar will survive the battle, as will the sons of Thor, Magni and Modi, and the god Hoenir. Balder and Hoder will be returned to life. Christianity made its mark on Norse mythology, too, and so it is recorded that, after Ragnarok, there will be the incarnation of a god too great to be named – in other words, Jahweh.

The Truth Behind
Some 'Myths'

Until a few decades ago it was assumed that the Viking myths were, without exception, nothing more than just that – myths. More recently, however, good evidence has appeared to show that some of the tales were firmly rooted in fact. The Saga of Eirik the Red tells of how this mighty warrior sailed from Scandinavia to discover a new country to the west, which he called 'Greenland' and where he founded a Viking colony around AD 985. This colony was not particularly successful, but it served as a launching post for the much more ambitious expedition of Eirik's son, Leif Eriksson, who sailed all the way across the Atlantic to found a colony, Vinland, on the eastern coast of North America. Remnants of this colony have now been found.

The Vikings also worked southwards, down to the Mediterranean, at one point – with the Irish Celts – even threatening the Roman Empire. In this context many of the 'myths' about the Vikings must be looked at very seriously indeed.

BELOW *Hjorleifshofdi, on the southern coast of Iceland, the first place where the Vikings established a settlement on that island.*

Iotun heimar.

D   E   F

Rise Land

Narve oe

MARE GLACIALE.

Biarmaland

GRÖNLANDIA

Huidserk

Herioifnes

Norvegia

Island

Ferøe

Frisland
H

Hetland

Helleland
G

Orcades

SIUR di Stephanii terrarum hyperborearü delineatio Año 1570

Markland

IRLAND

BRITANNIAL

Promontorium Wiinlandiæ

Skrælinge Land.
A
B

290   300   310   320   330   340   350   360   10   20

400   300   310   340   330   340   350   360   10   20

LEFT A 1590 version of
a map supposed to have
been compiled by
Sigurdur Stefánsson.
Although the scale is
lamentably awry
(possibly because of
copying and recopying
over the centuries), it is
clear that it is based on
knowledge rather than
guesswork.

TOP LEFT
Reconstruction of a Viking farm at Stong, Iceland.

BOTTOM LEFT *Interior of the Stong farm.*

RIGHT *A piece of modern sculpture at Bratahild shows representations of Viking symbols.*

RIGHT *Remains of a Viking church at Hvalsoe, Greenland.*

RIGHT *Part of the eastern coast of Newfoundland. It is on this coast that Leif Eriksson probably founded, around AD 1000, his short-lived colony called Vinland.*

FURTHER READING

Crossley-Holland, Kevin
The Norse Myths
London, Deutsch, 1980

Davidson, HR Ellis
Gods and Myths of Northern Europe
Harmondsworth, Penguin, 1964

Davidson, HR Ellis
Scandinavian Mythology
London, Hamlyn, revised edition 1982

Davidson, HR Ellis
The Viking Road to Byzantium
London, Allen & Unwin, 1976

Esping, Mikael
The Vikings
London, Piccolo, 1982

Green, Roger Lancelyn
Myths of the Norsemen
London, Puffin, 1970

Guerber, HA
Myths of the Norsemen
London, Harrap, 1908

Hveberg, Harald (translated Pat Shaw Iversen)
Of Gods and Giants
Oslo, Johan Grundt Tanum Forlag with the Office of Cultural Relations,
Norwegian Ministry of Foreign Affairs, 1961

Jones, Gwyn (translator and editor)
Eirik the Red and Other Icelandic Sagas
London, Oxford University Press, 1961

Sawyer, PH
The Age of the Vikings
London, Edward Arnold, second edition, 1971

Snorri Sturluson (translated by Jean I Young)
The Prose Edda
Cambridge, Bowes & Bowes, 1954

Index

127

Picture Credits

The Publishers would like to thank the following for supplying the illustrations for this book:

Canada Tourist Board (© Andrew Dawson): page 122 bottom.

CM Dixon, Canterbury: pages 6, 7, 8, 10, 11 top, 12, 13, 17, 18, 19, 20, 21, 23, 25, 28, 29, 30/31, 32, 33, 34, 35, 37, 38, 39, 41, 44, 45, 46, 50, 53, 56, 57, 58, 59, 64, 65, 66, 68, 69, 70, 71, 72, 75, 76/77, 80, 83, 84, 85, 88, 91, 94, 95, 97, 99, 100/101, 106/107, 108, 110/111, 113, 114, 116, 117 and 118.

The Danish Tourist Board: pages 24 and 79 (Wedigo Ferchland).

Mary Evans Picture Library: pages 14, 15, 16, 22, 42, 45 background, 47, 48, 51, 55, 60, 63, 73, 74, 78, 82, 89, 90, 96 and 98.

Iceland and Greenland Images: pages 26, 27, 36 (© IC Wilton), 86, 87, 109, 119, 121, 122 top, 124 and 123.

Det Kongelige Bibliotek, København: pages 11 bottom and 120.

The Mansell Collection: pages 92/93 and 103.

York Archaeological Trust: page 104.